EMOTIONS

CAN YOU TRUST THEM?

DR. JAMES DOBSON

Regal

A Division of Gospel Light
Ventura, California, U.S.A.

Published by Regal Books
A Division of Gospel Light
Ventura, California 93006
Printed in U.S.A.

Scripture quotations in this publication, unless otherwise indicated, are from the
New International Version, Holy Bible. Copyright © 1978 by New York International Bible Society. Used by permission. Other versions quoted are:

KJV—Authorized *King James Version.*

TLB—*The Living Bible*, Copyright © 1971 by Tyndale House Publishers, Wheaton, Illinois. Used by permission.

RSV—*Revised Standard Version* of the Bible, copyrighted 1946 and 1952 by the Division of Christian Education of the NCCC, U.S.A., and used by permission.

NEB—*The New English Bible.* © The Delegates of the Oxford University Press and The Syndics of the Cambridge University Press 1961, 1970. Reprinted by permission.

Phillips—*The New Testament in Modern English*, Revised Edition. J.B. Phillips, Translator. © J.B. Phillips 1958, 1960, 1972. Used by permission of Macmillan Publishing Co., Inc.

TEV—The *Good News Bible*, The Bible in Today's English Version. Old Testament copyright © American Bible Society, 1966. New Testament copyright © American Bible Society, 1966, 1971, 1976. Used by permission.

Mass edition, 1981

Library of Congress Catalog Card No. 79-91703
ISBN 0-8307-1672-6

8 9 10 11 12 13 14 / KP / 99 98 97

Rights for publishing this book in other languages are contracted by Gospel Literature International (GLINT). GLINT also provides technical help for the adaptation, translation, and publishing of Bible study resources and books in scores of languages worldwide. For further information, contact GLINT, Post Office Box 4060, Ontario, California, 91761-1003, U.S.A., or the publisher.

Contents

Contents

Introduction

Emotions in the Christian Life

You're about to read a book about human emotion and its impact on our daily lives. That topic always reminds me of a story my mother told about the high school she attended in 1930. It was located in a small Oklahoma town which had produced a series of terrible football teams. They usually lost the important games and were invariably clobbered by their arch rivals from a nearby community. Understandably, the students and their parents began to get depressed and dispirited by the drubbing their troops were given every Friday night. It must have been awful.

Finally, a wealthy oil producer decided to take matters in his own hands. He asked to speak to the team in the locker room after yet another devastating defeat. What followed was one of the most dramatic football speeches of all times. This businessman proceeded to offer a brand new Ford to every boy on the team and to each coach if they would simply defeat their bitter rivals in the next game. Knute Rockne couldn't have said it better.

The team went crazy with sheer delight. They howled and cheered and slapped each other on their padded behinds. For seven days, the boys ate, drank and breathed football. At night they dreamed about touchdowns and rumbleseats. The entire school caught the spirit of ecstasy, and a holiday fever pervaded the campus. Each player could visualize himself behind the wheel of a gorgeous coupe, with eight gorgeous girls hanging all over his gorgeous body.

Finally, the big night arrived and the team assembled in the locker room. Excitement was at an unprecedented high. The coach made several inane comments and the boys hurried out to face the enemy. They assembled on the sidelines, put their hands together and shouted a simultaneous "Rah!" Then they ran onto the field and were demolished, 38 to zero.

The team's exuberance did not translate into a single point on the scoreboard. Seven days of hoorah and whoop-de-do simply couldn't compensate for the players' lack of discipline and conditioning and practice and study and coaching and drill and experience and character. Such is the nature of emotion. It has a definite place in human affairs, but when forced to stand alone, feelings usually reveal themselves to be unreliable and ephemeral and even a bit foolish.[1]

On the other hand, it would be a mistake to minimize the impact of emotion on human behavior. I recently described this influence in my book, *Straight Talk to Men and Their Wives*, and have obtained permission to quote a section of that discussion as follows:

Have you ever stood outdoors near the end of a day and heard the whining sound of a mosquito flying past your ear?

"I'll bet I'm about to get punctured," you think.

Just then, you feel the creature light on your forearm and you immediately glance downward. But to your surprise, the insect is not there. You merely imagined that you had been invaded.

Or in another context, have you ever awakened after a frightening dream, lying breathless in your bed? You listened to the sounds of the night, wondering if the dream was based on reality. Then suddenly, just as you expected, there was a "bump" coming from the dark side of the house. An hour later you concluded that no one was actually there.

Emotions are powerful forces within the human mind. Fear, especially, has a remarkable way of generating evidence to support itself. Physicians in clinical practice spend a large portion of their time convincing people that their self-diagnoses are not accurate . . . that their symptoms are imaginary or psychosomatic.

Even the young and the brave experience such deception. My good friend, Steve Smith, won a bronze star for courage in Vietnam combat. However, the first night his unit arrived in the war torn country was not to be remembered for remarkable valor. His company had never seen actual combat, and the men were terrified. They dug foxholes on a hill and nervously watched the sun disappear beyond the horizon. At approximately midnight, the enemy attacked as anticipated. Guns began to blaze on one side of the mountain, and before long, all the soldiers were firing frantically and throwing hand grenades into the darkness. The battle raged throughout the night and the infantry appeared to be winning. Finally, the long awaited sun came up and the body count began. But not one single dead Viet Cong lay at the perimeter of the mountain. In fact, not one enemy soldier had even participated in the attack. The company of green troops had fought the night in mortal combat . . . and won!

Permit me one further example of emotions that overruled reason. The city of Los Angeles was paralyzed with fear in 1969, when Charles Manson and his "family" murdered Sharon Tate and her friends, and then butchered Leno and Rosemary La Bianca in cold blood. Residents wondered who would be next? My mother was quite convinced that she was the prime candidate. Sure enough, Mom and Dad heard the intruder as they lay in bed one night. "Thump!" went the sound from the area of the kitchen.

"Did you hear that?" asked my mother.

"Yes, be quiet," said my father.

They lay staring at the darkened ceiling, breathing shallowly and listening for further clues. A second "thump" brought them to their feet. They felt their way to the bedroom door which was closed. At this point, we are shown a vast difference between how my mother and my father faced a crisis. Her inclination was to hold the door shut to keep the intruder from entering the bedroom. Thus, she propped her foot against the bottom of the door and threw her weight against the upper section. My father's approach was to confront the attacker head on. He reached through the darkness and grasped the doorknob, but his pull met the resistance from my mother.

My father assumed someone was holding the door shut from the other side. My terrified mother, on the other hand, could feel the killer trying to force the door open. My parents stood there in the pitch blackness of midnight, struggling against one another and imagining themselves to be in a tug of war with a murderer. Mother then decided to abandon ship. She released the door and ran to the window to scream at the top of her lungs. She took a great breath of air with which to summon the entire city of Pasadena, when she realized a light was on behind her. Turning around, she saw that my Dad had gone into the other part of the house in search of their attacker. Obviously, he was able to open the door when she released it. In reality there was no prowler. The thumps were never identified and Charles Manson never made his anticipated visit.

Let me personalize the issue at hand. What imaginary fears are *you* supporting with contrived evidence? What role do rampant emotions play in your life? It is likely that what you feel, right or wrong, is a pervasive force in determining your behavior day by day. Emotional experience in the western world has become *the* primary motivation of values and actions and even spiritual beliefs. Furthermore, (and this is the point), we are living in a day when people are being encouraged to release their emotions, to grant them even greater power in ruling their destinies. We are told, "if it feels good, do it!" The popular song, "You Light Up My Life," carries this phrase, "It can't be wrong, 'cause it *feels* so right." (Hitler's murder of the Jews probably felt right to the Nazis at the time). Most love songs, in fact, make it clear that a commitment to one another is based on the excitement the couple shares. Thus, when the thrill evaporates, so goes the relationship. By contrast, the greatest piece of literature ever written on the subject of love, the 13th Chapter of I Corinthians, includes not a single reference to feelings: "Love is very patient and kind, never jealous or envious, never boastful or proud, never haughty or selfish or rude. Love does not demand its own way. It is not irritable or touchy. It does not hold grudges and will hardly even notice when others do it wrong." (1 Corinthians 13:4-5 TLB)

It is my opinion that we should take a long, hard look at the "discovery of personhood," which seeks to free our emotions from restraint and inhibition. The pop-psyche movement, so prevalent in San Francisco and other California cities, encourages us to get in touch with our feelings . . . to open up . . . to tell it like it is. We've come through an emphasis on "encounter groups," where participants were urged to attack one another and cry and scream and remove their clothes and even whack each other with foamy "encounter bats." Great stuff.

I have no desire to return our culture to the formality of yesterday, when father was a marble statue and mother couldn't smile because her corset was too tight. But if our grandparents represented one extreme of emotional repression, today's Americans have become temperamental yo-yos at the other. We live and breathe by the vicissitudes of our feelings, and for many, the depression of the "lows" is significantly more prevalent than the elation of the "highs." Reason is now *dominated* by feelings, rather than the reverse as God intended. "But when the Holy Spirit controls our lives he will produce this kind of fruit in us: love, joy, peace, patience, kindness, goodness, faithfulness, gentleness and *self-control.*" (Galations 5:22 TLB)

This need for *self-control* is emphasized by the difficulties and stresses that occur in the lives of virtually every human being on earth. As Mark Twain said, "Life is just one darn thing after another" It's true. At least once every two weeks, someone gets a chest cold or the roof springs a leak or the car throws a rod or an ingrown toenail becomes infected or a business crisis develops. Those minor frustrations are inevitable. In time, of course, more significant problems develop. Loved ones die and catastrophic diseases appear and life slowly grinds to a conclusion. This is the nature of human experience, like it or not. That being true, nothing could be more dangerous than to permit our emotions to rule our destinies. To do so is to be cast adrift in the path of life's storms.[2]

This statement was intended to convey one primary message: emotions must always be accountable to the faculties of reason and will. That accountability is doubly important for those of us who purport to be Christians. If we are to be defeated during life's spiritual pilgrimage, it is likely that negative emotions will play a dominant role in that discouragement. Satan is devastatingly effective in using the weapons of guilt, rejection, fear, embarrassment, grief, depression, loneliness and misunderstanding. Indeed, human beings are vulnerable creatures who could not withstand these satanic pressures without divine assistance.

Someone wrote, "The mind, body and soul are very close neighbors, and one usually catches the ills of the others." I agree. A person who experiences deep feelings of inferiority, for example, usually believes that God disrespects him too. Consider this note written by a small boy to a famous psychotherapist:

Dear Docter Gardner

What is bothering me is that long ago some big person it is a boy about 13 years old. He called me turtle and I knew he said that because of my plastic sergery.

And I think god hates me because of my lip. And when I die he'll probably send me to hell.

Love, Chris[3]

Chris had obviously drawn the conclusion that since he was worthless, not even God could love him. It was an illogical extrapolation, yet emotions are not bound by principles of logic. He *felt* hated by God. That same lie has been whispered in the ears of a million Christians who are overwhelmed by inadequacy and inferiority. Likewise, *every* river of emotion running deep within the human spirit has the capacity of overflowing its banks and flooding the mind with its rampaging waters. That is why I have written the pages of this book. Our purpose has been to fortify the banks of those rivers with scriptural truth and psychological understanding.

At least eight or ten specific emotions could have been addressed in this context. However, the limitations of time and space required us to focus on four of the most important. They are as follows:

1. *Guilt*
    a. When is it valid and invalid, and how can the difference be known?
    b. What are the consequences of false guilt which can never be "forgiven"?

   c. What is the origin of the conscience, and can it be trusted?

   d. Can parents influence the consciences of their children, and if so, how should they be taught?

   e. Does the absence of guilt mean we are blameless before God?

2. *Romantic Love*

   a. How can the "feeling of love" become a dangerous trap?

   b. Why do so many couples become disillusioned shortly after the honeymoon?

   c. Does "love at first sight" ever occur?

   d. Does God select one particular person for us to marry and then guide us together?

   e. How can love be kept alive?

3. *Anger*

   a. Is all "anger" sinful?

   b. How can strong negative feelings be handled without violating scriptural principles and without repressing them into the unconscious mind?

   c. Is it possible for the Christian to live without feelings of irritation or hostility?

   d. Does being morally "right" in a particular instance justify an attitude of resentment and antagonism?

   e. What is the "flight or fight" mechanism, and how does it relate to biblical understandings?

4. *Interpreting Our Impressions*

   a. Can we trust our impressions in interpreting the will of God?

b. Under what circumstances does God speak directly to the heart of man?

c. Does Satan also speak directly on occasion? If so, how can the two voices be distinguished?

d. What role does fatigue and illness play in the interpretation of impressions?

e. How can major decisions be made without leaning too heavily on ephemeral emotions?

Following each part is a section, "Learning-Discussion Ideas." The objective is to permit the material to be used in Sunday School classes, neighborhood Bible study classes, or any other setting where it might be beneficial. Since virtually every human being has dealt with these common emotions at some point, it is often helpful to share experiences with sympathetic friends and fellow Christians. In other instances individuals will be able to use the reference pages personally.

As we approach the first topic of *guilt,* let me leave you with a Scripture which assures us that we need not be victims of our own emotions. The God who created the vast resources of the universe is also the inventor of the human mind. His inspired words of encouragement guarantee us that we can live above our circumstances.

"I have learned to be satisfied with what I have. I know what it is to be in need, and what it is to have more than enough. I have learned this secret, so that anywhere, at any time, I am content, whether I am full or hungry, whether I have too much or too little. I have the strength to face all conditions by the power that Christ gives me (Phil. 4:11-13, *TEV*).

Notes

1. This inability of emotion to stand alone may explain the short duration of the "Jesus Movement," which flourished briefly in the 1960s. Young people entered into a highly emotional relationship with the Creator, but had little theological or scriptural understanding to give it substance. Thus, some who became such enthusiastic new Christians were soon experimenting with various sects and cults and religions. To quote the previous statement, "Hoorah and whoop-de-do can't compensate for an absence of discipline and conditioning and practice and study and coaching and drill and experience and character."

2. James C. Dobson, *Straight Talk to Men and Their Wives* (Waco, TX: Word, Inc., 1980).

3. James Dobson, *Hide or Seek* (Old Tappan, NJ: Fleming H. Revell Co., 1974), p. 48.

PART I
Guilt

- When is it valid and invalid, and how can the difference be known?
- What are the consequences of false guilt which can never be "forgiven"?
- What is the origin of the conscience, and can it be trusted?
- Can parents influence the consciences of their children, and if so, how should they be taught?
- Does the absence of guilt mean we are blameless before God?

GUILT: THE PAINFUL EMOTION

Few human emotions are as distressing and painful as feelings of guilt and personal disapproval. When at a peak of intensity, self-condemnation gnaws on the conscious mind by day and invades the dreams by night. Since the voice of the conscience speaks from inside the human mind, we cannot escape its unrelenting abuse for our mistakes, failures and sins. For some particularly vulnerable individuals, an internal taskmaster is on the job from early morning until late at night—screaming accusations at his tormented victim. Hospitals for the emotionally disturbed are filled with such patients who have been unable to meet their own expectations and are now broken with self-blame and even personal hatred.

But is all guilt harmful? Certainly not. Feelings of personal disapproval can provide powerful motivation for responsible behavior. A husband may go to work when he would rather go fishing, simply because he knows his wife and children need the money and he would feel guilty if he ignored his family obligations. Dr. William Glasser, psychiatrist and author of *Reality Therapy*, asserts that personal disapproval for wrong behavior is absolutely necessary if change for the better is to occur. Perhaps the best example of this principle is seen in a religious conversion experience. Genuine repentance occurs only when we recognize our sorrowful condition and bow at the feet of Jesus Christ.

How, then, are we to make sense out of our feelings of guilt? How can we separate destructive self-condemnation from the genuine accusations of God? In the following discussion we will examine some of the related issues to gain a better understanding of this powerful emotion which surges within each of us.

THE ORIGIN OF GUILT

What causes a person to feel guilty?

A poll was taken among children ages 5 through 9 on the question, "What is a conscience?" One 6-year-old girl said a conscience is the spot inside that "burns if you're not good." A 6-year-old boy said he didn't know, but thought it had something to do with feeling bad when you "kicked girls or little dogs." And a 9-year-old explained it as a voice inside that says "No" when you want to do something like beating up your little brother. Her conscience had "saved him a lot of times!"

Adults have also found the conscience difficult to define. I tend to believe that a sense of guilt occurs when we violate our own inner code of conduct. Guilt is a message of disapproval from the conscience which says, in effect, "You should be ashamed of yourself!"

If guilt conveys a message from our consciences and the conscience was created by God—then, is it accurate to say that guilt feelings always contain a message of disapproval from God, too?

Let me give you an illustration of a young man who struggled with guilt, and then you indicate the role you think God played in his condemnation.

Some friends of mine decided to take a two-week

vacation one summer, and they hired a 15-year-old boy (whom I'll call John) to water their lawn and bring in the mail while they were gone. They gave him a key to their house and asked him to maintain their property until they returned.

John did the job satisfactorily and was paid for his efforts. Some months later, however, he came to their house again and knocked on the front door. He stood there, obviously shaken with emotion, saying he had something important to tell them. My friends invited John into the living room, where he confessed that he had entered their house one day to bring in the mail, and had seen a stick of gum lying on a table. He stole the gum and chewed it, but had suffered intense guilt ever since. The weeping young man then took a penny from his pocket and asked them to accept it as repayment for the stolen gum, requesting their forgiveness for his dishonesty.

Now, what do you think was the origin of his remorseful guilt? Was God actually condemning this sensitive adolescent, or was the disapproval of his own making? More specifically, let's suppose *you* were counseling John and he asked you whether he should return the penny and confess, or whether he should ask God to forgive him and forget it ever happened.

What is your interpretation of John's struggle? I have presented the illustration of John to several groups of Christian adults, and their reaction has been extremely varied. Some individuals feel that the conscience is largely a product of early childhood instruction, and John had obviously been taught to be super-sensitive to the voice within. Perhaps his parents or a minister had made him feel guilty over behaviors which would not ordinarily have distressed him. Those who took this position, therefore, were inclined to emphasize the human factors involved, while minimizing the voice of God in his experience.

Other discussants interpreted John's behavior very differently. They pointed out the fact that stealing is stealing, and the size of the theft is irrelevant to the issue at hand. Taking something that doesn't belong to you is a sin, regardless of whether you confiscate a stick of gum or a new automobile. Representatives of this point of view believe that John deserved the guilt he felt and should have made the restitution at my friend's home. To them, God was the author of the young man's guilt.

As to my personal views of John's predicament, I believe he did the right thing in confessing the theft as he did. If he suppressed his guilt in this instance, it would be easier to ignore the effects of greater misbehaviors in the future. Young children who pilfer things from a counter— one cent at a time—can easily progress to full-fledged shoplifting and more serious acts of dishonesty. From this perspective John's guilt appears valid and worthy of restitution.

While I view this young man's responsiveness to right and wrong as a healthy characteristic, I have some concern for his spiritual welfare in the future. A person with a tender conscience, such as John, is often vulnerable to a particular kind of satanic influence. By setting an ethical standard which is impossible to maintain, Satan can generate severe feelings of condemnation and spiritual discouragement. This brings us back to the question before us relating to the origin of guilt. Let me state with the strongest emphasis that

God is *not* the author of all such discomfort. Some feelings of guilt are obviously inspired by the devil and have nothing to do with the commandments, values or judgments of our Creator.

Would you give some examples of a guilty conscience which God does not inspire? Can a person really feel crushing disapproval and yet be blameless before God?

Categorically, yes! I serve on the Attending Staff for Children's Hospital of Los Angeles in the Division of Medical Genetics. We see children throughout the year who are victims of various metabolic problems, most of which cause mental retardation in our young patients. Furthermore, most of these medical problems are produced by genetic errors—that is, each parent contributed a defective gene at the moment of conception which resulted in an unhealthy child. When a mother and father realize that they are individually responsible for the distorted, broken, intellectually damaged child before them, the impact can be disastrous. A sense of guilt sweeps over some parents in such enormous quantities that the family is destroyed.

Now, it is obvious that God is not the author of this kind of disapproval. He knows—even better than we—that the grief-stricken parents did not intentionally produce a defective child. Their genetic system simply malfunctioned. Certainly our merciful Creator would not hold them responsible for a consequence which they could not have anticipated or avoided. Nevertheless, the guilt is often unbearable for parents who hold *themselves* personally responsible.

Parenthood itself can be a very guilt-producing affair. Even when we give it our best effort, we can see our own failures and mistakes reflected in the lives of our children. We in the Western world are extremely vulnerable to family-related guilt. One mother whom I know walked toward a busy street with her three-year-old daughter. The little toddler ran ahead and stopped on the curb until her mother told her it was safe to cross. The woman was thinking about something else and nodded in approval when the little child asked, "Can I go now, Mommy?"

The youngster ran into the street and was struck full force by a semi-trailer truck. The mother gasped in terror as she watched the front and back wheels of the truck crush the life from her precious little girl. The hysterical woman, screaming in anguish and grief, ran to the road and gathered the broken remains of the child in her arms. She had killed her own daughter who depended on her for safety. This mother will *never* escape the guilt of that moment. The "video tape recording" has been rerun a million times in her tormented mind—picturing a trusting baby asking her mother if it was safe to cross the street. Clearly, God has not placed that guilt on the heartbroken woman, but her suffering is no less real.

I could give many other examples of severe guilt which were seemingly self-inflicted or imposed by circumstances.

Would you explain your statement that a sense of guilt is sometimes inspired by Satan?

Second Corinthians 11:14 indicates that Satan presents himself as "an angel of light," meaning he speaks as a false representative of God. Accordingly, it has been my

observation that undeserved guilt is one of the most powerful weapons in the devil's arsenal. By seeming to ally
himself with the voice of the Holy Spirit, Satan uses the
conscience to accuse, torment and berate his victims.
What better tool for spiritual discouragement could there
be than feelings of guilt which cannot be "forgiven"—
because they do not represent genuine disapproval from
God?

I met a young man who was extremely sensitive to the
voice of his conscience. He wanted nothing more than to
serve God, and toward this end he accepted every impression or feeling as though it had been sent directly from the
Lord. Nevertheless, he still felt remorse at each point of
imperfection. He was "living by the law" in this sense, but
his personal standards were far more rigorous than the Ten
Commandments. If he saw some glass on a sidewalk but
failed to remove it, he felt guilty for having caused a
possible wound to a child. This compulsion extended into
every area of his life, creating discomfort for the things he
owned, or anything which gave him pleasure. And, of
course, his inability to stifle every inappropriate sexual
impulse created further agitation.

This young man (we'll call him Walt) felt he could only
be justified in the sight of God by balancing each of his evil
acts by a corresponding good deed. Unfortunately, the
"sin" occurred faster than his "atonement." In fear that he
would forget his misdeeds and errors, he began to write
them down. Walt would sit in church and describe his sins
on the sides of bulletins and visitors' cards.

Despite his best efforts to be perfect, however, he fell
farther and farther behind in the obligation to counterbal-

ance his innumerable misdeeds. His constant sensation of guilt then began to generate theological confusion and spiritual discouragement. There was simply no way to satisfy his angry and demanding Creator.

Through a process of rationalization and emotional crises, Walt's faith and spiritual commitment were finally extinguished. Consequently, this young man is solidly entrenched in atheism today. He has, I believe, shielded himself from the agitation of guilt by denying the existence of the God who had accused him of so many unavoidable "sins."

The Bible describes Satan as being enormously cunning and vicious. He is not at all like the comical character depicted in popular literature, with a pitchfork and pointed tail. He is a "roaring lion, looking for someone to devour" (see 1 Pet. 5:8). In fact, he is a threat even to those whom God has elected and received as His own. Thus, it has been my observation that <u>Satan does not give up on the</u> committed Christian—he merely attacks from a different direction. In the case of Walt, he destroyed this young man's faith by flogging him with "unforgivable" guilt.

You have shown that some guilt does not come from the judgment of God. In other words, one can feel guilty when he is innocent before God. Now, how about the opposite side of that coin. Does the absence of guilt mean we are blameless in the sight of the Creator? Can I depend on my conscience to let me know when God is displeased with me?

Apparently, not always. There are many examples of vicious, evil people who seem to feel no guilt for their actions. We can't know for sure, of course, but there is no evidence that Adolph Hitler experienced any serious measure of self-condemnation toward the end of his life, despite the torment he had inflicted on the world.

How could he withstand the knowledge that, at his order, hundreds of thousands of innocent Jewish children were torn from the arms of their screaming parents and thrown into gas chambers or shot by SS troops? In 1944, when the Allied armies were closing in on Germany, thousands of naked children and babies were exposed to snowstorms and doused with water to cause their deaths by freezing. Hitler conceived and implemented this horrible "final solution," but he is never known to have uttered a word of self-doubt or remorse.

Likewise, Joseph Stalin is said to have murdered between 20 and 30 million people during his long dictatorship, yet, his conscience apparently remained quiet and unprovoked to the end. There was no obvious deathbed repentance or regret.

My point is that the voice of disapproval from within is a fragile thing in some people. It can be seared and ignored until its whisper of protest is heard no longer. Perhaps the most effective silencer for the conscience is found in widespread social opinions. If everybody is doing it—the reasoning goes—it can't be very harmful or sinful.

One study reveals that 66 percent of today's college students now feel it is okay (i.e., not guilt producing) to have sexual intercourse with someone they have dated and "like a lot." One quarter of all individuals of college age have shared a bedroom with a member of the opposite sex for three months or more. You see, if these same "liberated" young people had participated in that kind of sexual behavior 20 years ago, most of them would have had to deal with feelings of guilt and remorse. But now, however, they are lulled into a false sense of security by the fact that their behavior is socially acceptable. Individual guilt is partially a product of collective attitudes and concepts of morality, despite the fact that God's standards are eternal and are not open to revision or negotiation. His laws will remain in force even if the whole world rejects them, as in the days of Noah.

I am saying that the conscience is an imperfect mental faculty. There are times when it condemns us for mistakes and human frailties that can't be avoided; at other times it will remain silent in the face of indescribable wickedness.

LIVING WITH CONSCIENCE

What am I to do with my conscience then? Is it to be ignored altogether? Does God not speak through this mental faculty?

Let's turn to the Scripture for answers to those questions. Direct reference is made to the conscience in dozens of passages throughout the Word. I have listed a few of those references, as follows, where the Authorized *King James Version* of the Bible refers to—

- a "weak conscience" 1 Corinthians 8:7
- a "defiled conscience" Titus 1:15
- a "conscience void of offense" Acts 24:16
- a "pure conscience" 1 Timothy 3:9
- a "good conscience" Acts 23:1; Hebrews 13:18
- a "conscience seared with a hot iron" 1 Timothy 4:2

- a "conscience bearing witness" Romans 2:15
- the "testimony of our conscience" 2 Corinthians 1:12
- the "answer of a good conscience toward God" 1 Peter 3:21.

We simply cannot deny the existence of the conscience or the fact that the Holy Spirit influences us through it. Especially pertinent to this point is Romans 9:1, "I am speaking the truth as a Christian, and my own conscience, enlightened by the Holy Spirit, assures me it is no lie" (*NEB*).

Another Scripture which puts the conscience in proper perspective is found in Romans 2:14, and is quoted as follows: "When the gentiles, who have no knowledge of the Law, act in accordance with it by the light of nature, they show that they have a law in *themselves*, for they demonstrate the effect of a law operating in their own hearts. Their *own consciences endorse the existence of such a law, for there is something which condemns or excuses their actions*" (*Phillips*, italics added.)

There it is in definite terms. The conscience is reality, and the Holy Spirit makes use of it. On the other hand, the conscience has been shown to be unreliable on occasions. That contradiction poses a difficult dilemma for us as Christians; we must lean to separate the true from the untrue, the real from the imagined, the right from wrong. How can we discern, for sure, the pleasure and displeasure of our loving God when the voice from within is somewhat unpredictable?

You are obviously not suggesting that we ignore our consciences altogether, are you?

Most certainly not. As we have seen, the conscience is often specifically illuminated by the Holy Spirit and we *must* not disregard His leadings. My words to this point could offer ammunition for the confirmed rationalizer who wants to do his own thing anyway. However, my purpose is not to weaken the importance of the conscience, but rather to help us interpret its meaning more effectively.

Guilt is an expression of the conscience which is a product of our emotions. It is a *feeling* of disapproval which is conveyed to the rational mind by what we might call the "Department of the Emotions." Working steadily in the Department of the Emotions is the "Internal Committee on Ethics and Morality"—a group of stern little fellows who review all of our actions and attitudes. Nothing that we do escapes their attention, and they can be most offensive when they observe a difference between the way things are and the way they ought to be. However, the condemnation that they issue (and even their approval) is subject to error; they are biased by what they have seen and heard, and they sometimes make mistakes. Therefore, before the judgment of the Committee on E. & M. is accepted as Truth, it must be tested within two other "departments" of the mind. The emotion of condemnation cannot be ignored, but it shouldn't be allowed to stand unchallenged, either.

Thus, a *feeling of guilt* must be referred to the "Department of the Intellect" for further evaluation and confirmation. There it is tested against rational criteria: What does my pastor recommend? What does my own judgment say about the behavior in question? Is it reasonable that God would hold me responsible for what I've done or thought?

And, of course, the ultimate standard on which guilt is evaluated must be the Holy Scripture. What does the Bible say on the matter? If it is not directly mentioned, what underlying principle is implied? In this way, guilt is evaluated for its validity according to the intellectual process of reason.

There will be times when guilt will originate not in the emotions, but in the intellect itself. Suppose a person is studying the Bible and reads Jesus' words, "All liars will have their place in the lake of fire" (see Rev. 21:8). He immediately remembers his distorted income tax return, and the numerous "white lies" he has told. The matter is instantaneously referred to the "Department of Emotions" and guilt ensues.

But there is a third division of the mind which must review the decisions of the emotions and the intellect. It is called the "Department of the Will." This is a vitally important mental faculty, for it deals with the person's intent. I personally believe no guilt should be considered to have come from God unless the behavior was an expression of willful disobedience.

Let me explain my point. Suppose I gave my three-year-old son a direct order: "Ryan, please close the door." However, in his childish immaturity he failed to grasp the meaning of my words and opened the door further. He did not obey me. He did the exact opposite of what I commanded. Yet I would be a most unworthy father if I punished him for his failure. He was trying to do what I asked, but his understanding of my request was incomplete. You see, I judge my son more by his *intent* than by his actual behavior. Accordingly, Ryan is never so likely to be punished as when he knows what I want and he refuses to obey me.

It is with great comfort that I rest in that same relationship with God. I am certain that there are times when I do the opposite of what He wants. In my humanness—in my partial understanding—I undoubtedly fall short of His best for my life. But I believe that my merciful Father judges me according to the expression of my will. When He has told me what He requires and I refuse to obey, I stand without excuse before Him.

The character of God is illustrated in the person of Jesus, whose death on the Roman cross is relevant to our discussion. Few of us can imagine the agony of death by crucifixion. (The only way a victim could exhale on the cross was to push upward on his nail-pierced feet—which explains why death inevitably followed the breaking of the legs.)

Despite the horrible pain and torment which Jesus was enduring above the crowd which mocked and ridiculed Him, He looked down upon the executioners and said, "Father, forgive them." Why? "*For they do not know what they are doing*" (Luke 23:34). He did not hold them personally responsible for the most dastardly crime in the history of mankind, because they were following military orders and did not knowingly—willfully—defy God. It is my firm conviction that Jesus offers me that same mercy. Psalm 103:13 indicates that He pities us as a father pities his children. That is an analogy I can understand!

To summarize this viewpoint, let me say again that the feeling of guilt is important and must not be ignored. However, before it is accepted as a statement of divine disapproval, it must be tested in the intellect and in the will. The chart that follows depicts this process.

Mental Faculty	Test
1. Emotion	What do I feel?
2. Intellect	Is it reasonable and biblical?
3. Will	What was my intent?

When we stand culpable before God Almighty, guilt will be validated by all three "departments" of the mind. In some ways, they operate as a system of checks and balances—as was intended for the executive, legislative and judicial branches of the United States Government. Each division interacts with the work of the other two and keeps them from gaining unhealthy predominance. Accordingly, when the emotions are given a free hand, as in the experience of Walt, then an internal dictatorship is inevitable and guilt will flow like a wild river!

Would you give an example of a feeling of guilt which was subjected to the tests of intellect and will?

An incident from my own experience will illustrate the testing process I've suggested.

Several years ago my wife and I bought our first home, which was small but adequate for the two of us. When our daughter was born the following year, however, we felt it necessary to construct a family room. Fortunately, the man who had owned the house before us had entertained the same idea, and had built the roof and poured a concrete floor before abandoning the project. I hired a carpenter to enclose the walls and finish the interior of the room.

When the construction began, I was advised by my weekend builder (who was employed full time in another line of work) to avoid getting a building permit. He said that it would only make my taxes go up and was probably unnecessary. He was telling me just what I wanted to hear. I convinced myself that it was probably not mandatory to inform the city about my project primarily because I was not changing the square footage under the roof line. It was, as they say, a bloody rationalization.

I had my way and the new room was completed on schedule. The city was none the wiser and I settled the moral issue and laid it to rest. But it wouldn't stay down. When the property tax bill arrived the following spring, I could think only of the additional assessment I should have been paying for having improved my home. I argued down the guilt once again, but with greater effort than before. Then when the county assessor came by that summer, I watched him reevaluate my property from the street. He didn't look at the back of the house because he had no way of knowing anything new had been constructed there. That did it! For the first time, I faced the guilt squarely and subjected it to the tests of the intellect and will.

Failing to comply with city and county ordinances couldn't be right or honest. In a sense, I was stealing the difference between my lower tax bill and the amount it should have been. The Bible was abundantly clear on the issue of thievery. My guilt stood firm against all intellectual criteria.

The clincher occurred in the test of my will. I had to admit to myself that from the beginning I had known of the legal requirement to get a building permit. Despite my careful rationalization, I had willfully disobeyed the law. My guilt emerged intact.

The following day I sat down and wrote a letter to the county assessor. Explaining the whole story in detail, I provided the date of the construction and invited his representative to reevaluate the worth of my house. The sense of condemnation and blame seemed to flow from the end of my pen and was gone by the time I finished the letter. I asked God to forgive me and the issue was laid to rest—forever.

Incidentally, the county assessor receives a million letters a year from people who are complaining about their taxes being too high. I doubt if he has ever gotten a letter from someone asserting that his taxes were too low! He must have been completely unequipped to handle my note because he sent me a form letter telling me how I could appeal my exorbitant taxes if I was convinced I had been cheated. That was not exactly what I had in mind.

PARENTAL TRAINING OF THE CONSCIENCE

Would you describe more completely the nature of the conscience and how it functions? You implied earlier that a person's sense of guilt is dependent, in part, on what he was taught in childhood. Is that correct?

The subject of the conscience is an extremely complex and weighty topic. Philosophers and theologians have struggled with its meaning for centuries and their views have been characterized by disharmony and controversy from the beginning. Since I am neither a philosopher nor a theologian, I am keenly aware of the deep water in which we tread and have attempted to focus my views on the psychological aspects of the topic.

Concerning influences of childhood instruction on the conscience, the great German philosopher, Immanuel Kant, strongly opposed that concept. He stated un-equivocally that the conscience was *not* the product of experience but was an inherited capacity of the soul. I believe most child psychologists today would strongly dis-agree with Kant on this point. A person's conscience is largely a gift from his parents—from their training and instruction and approval and disapproval. The way that right and wrong are taught throughout the first decade of life will never be completely forgotten—even though it may be contradicted later.

That obviously places a tremendous responsi-bility on us as parents, doesn't it?

The proper "programming" of the conscience is one of the most difficult jobs associated with parenthood, and the one that requires the greatest wisdom. Fifty years ago, parents were more likely to produce excessive guilt in their children. Now, I feel, we have gone much too far in the other direction—in some cases teaching that nothing is sinful or harmful.

Shouldn't a child be allowed to decide for him-self on matters related to his concept of God?

Aren't we forcing our religion down his throat when we tell him what he must believe?

I was once asked this very question by a Christian parent. I responded in my book, *Dare to Discipline*, as follows:

Let me answer that question with an illustration from nature. A little gosling (baby goose) has a peculiar characteristic that is relevant at this point. Shortly after he hatches from his shell he will become attached, or "imprinted," to the first thing that he sees moving near him. From that time forward, he will follow that particular object when it moves in his vicinity. Ordinarily, he becomes imprinted to the mother goose who was on hand to hatch the new generation. If she is removed, however, the gosling will settle for any mobile substitute, whether alive or not. In fact, a gosling will become imprinted most easily to a blue football bladder, dragged by on a string. A week later, he'll fall in line behind the bladder as it scoots by him. Time is the critical factor in this process. The gosling is vulnerable to imprinting for only a few seconds after he hatches from the shell; if that opportunity is lost, it cannot be regained later. In other words, there is a critical, brief period in the life of the gosling when this instinctual learning is possible.

There is also a critical period when certain kinds of instruction are possible in the life of the child. Although humans have no instincts (only drives, reflexes, urges, etc.), there is a brief period during childhood when youngsters are vulnerable to religious training. Their concepts of right and wrong, which Freud called the superego, are formulated during this time, and their view of God begins to solidify. As in the case of the gosling, the opportunity of that period must be seized when it is available. Leaders of the Catholic Church have been widely quoted as saying, "Give us a child until he is seven years old and we'll have him for life"; their affirmation is usually correct, because permanent attitudes can be instilled during these seven vulnerable years. Unfortunately, however, the opposite is also true. The absence or misapplication of instruction through that prime-time period may place a severe limitation on the depth of the child's later devotion to God. When parents say they are going to withhold indoctrination from their small child, allowing him to "decide for himself," they are almost guaranteeing that he will "decide" in the negative. If a parent wants his child to have a meaningful faith, he must give up any misguided attempts at objectivity. The child listens closely to discover just how much his parent believes what he is preaching; any indecision or ethical confusion from the parent is likely to be magnified in the child.[1]

If those early years are so important, why is it that some children grow up to reject God, even though they have been raised in Christian homes and exposed to church services and religious instruction?

It is true that some adults display no appreciation or understanding of the values their parents thought they had taught them. To their utter dismay, Mom and Dad learn too late that their training just didn't take.

Each time I see this occur, I am reminded of the story of Eli in the Old Testament (see 1 Sam. 2—4). The devoted priest failed to save his own boys, both of whom became profane and evil young men. What disturbs me more, however, is that the saintly Samuel—one of the greatest men in the Bible—witnessed Eli's mistakes, yet proceeded to lose his children, too!

The message is loud and clear to me: God will not necessarily save our children as a reward for our own devotion! Christianity is not inherited by the next generation. We must do our early homework.

While parents have been commanded to "train up a child in the way he should go," this poses a critical question: What way *should* he go? If the first seven years represent the prime time for religious training, what should be taught during this period? What experiences should be included? What values should be emphasized?

It is my strong belief that a child should be exposed to a carefully conceived, systematic program of religious training. Yet we are much too haphazard about this matter. Perhaps we would hit the mark more often if we more clearly recognized the precise *target*.

A checklist for parents—*a set of targets at which to aim*—is included in the next few pages. Many of the items require maturity which children lack, and we should not try to make adult Christians out of our immature youngsters. But we can gently nudge them toward these goals—these targets—during the impressionable years of childhood.

Essentially, the six scriptural concepts that follow provide the foundation on which all future doctrine and faith will rest. They comprise, in effect, the substance of the conscience. Christian parents can use these six concepts as broad guidelines in the nurturing of their children.[2]

CONCEPT I—*Love the Lord your God with all your heart* (Mark 12:30).

_____ Is your child learning of the love of God through the love, tenderness and mercy of his parents? (Most important.)

_____ Is he learning to talk about the Lord, and to include Him in his thoughts and plans?

_____ Is he learning to turn to Jesus for help whenever he is frightened or anxious or lonely?

_____ Is he learning to read the Bible?

_____ Is he learning to pray?

_____ Is he learning the meaning of faith and trust?

_____ Is he learning the joy of the Christian way of life?

_____ Is he learning the beauty of Jesus' birth and death?

CONCEPT II—*Love your neighbor as yourself* (Mark 12:31).

_____ Is he learning to understand and empathize with the feelings of others?

_____ Is he learning not to be selfish and demanding?

_____ Is he learning to share?

_____ Is he learning how to be kind to others?

_____ Is he learning to accept *himself?*

CONCEPT III—*Teach me to do your will, for you are my God* (Ps. 143:10).

_____ Is he learning to obey his parents as preparation for later obedience to God? (Most important.)

_____ Is he learning to behave properly in church—God's house?

_____ Is he learning a healthy appreciation for both aspects of God's nature: love and justice?

_____ Is he learning to cooperate with, and submit to, authorities outside of self: parents, teachers, policemen, etc.?

_____ Is he learning the meaning of sin and its inevitable consequences?

CONCEPT IV—*Fear God and keep his commandments, for this is the whole duty of man* (Eccles. 12:13).

_____ Is he learning to be truthful and honest?

_____ Is he learning to keep the Sabbath day holy?

_____ Is he learning the relative insignificance of materialism?

_____ Is he learning the meaning of the Christian family, and the faithfulness to it which God intends?

CONCEPT V—*But the fruit of the Spirit is . . . self-control* (Gal. 5:22,23).

_____ Is he learning to give a portion of his allowance (and other money) to God?

_____ Is he learning to control his impulses?

_____ Is he learning to work and carry responsibility?

_____ Is he learning to tolerate minor frustration?

_____ Is he learning to memorize and quote Scripture?

CONCEPT VI—*He who humbles himself will be exalted* (Luke 14:11).

_____ Is he learning a sense of appreciation?

_____ Is he learning to thank God for the good things in his life?

_____ Is he learning to forgive and forget?

_____ Is he learning the vast difference between self-worth and egotistical pride?

_____ Is he learning to bow reverently before the God of the universe?

In conclusion, your child's first seven years should prepare him to say at the age of accountability, "Here am I, Lord, send me!" A properly informed conscience is the key to that preparation.

EIGHT CONCLUSIONS ABOUT GUILT

Let me summarize this brief discussion of guilt by restating the eight conclusions that I have drawn about this important topic. They are as follows:

1. God is not the author of all feelings of guilt.

2. The absence of guilt feelings does not necessarily mean we are blameless before God.

3. Therefore, the conscience is not absolutely valid in its representation of divine approval and disapproval.

4. However, Romans 9:1 teaches that the conscience is a tool of the Holy Spirit and is often enlightened by Him.

5. The conscience, then, is a valuable asset to the Christian rather than a defect to be overcome. We must interpret its messages with greater perceptiveness.

6. When feelings of guilt are reflective of God's disapproval, they can be validated by the test of the intellect and the will.

7. The conscience is largely a gift of one's parents, which places a tremendous responsibility on mothers and fathers to handle that assignment judiciously.

8. Regardless of what we feel, the ultimate test of one's acceptability to our Lord is found in Romans 8:1:

"There is therefore now no condemnation to them which are in Christ Jesus, who walk not after the flesh, but after the Spirit" (*KJV*).

LEARNING-DISCUSSION IDEAS

The Origin of Guilt

1. Read Dr. Dobson's comments on the "inner code of conduct" and its part in guilty feelings. List three things your inner code of conduct definitely labels *wrong*. Discuss with another person what kinds of experiences helped you develop your personal inner code of conduct. In a sentence describe a time when you felt guilty. Can you identify what in your personal code of conduct was violated to produce the guilty feelings?

2. Dr. Dobson gives an example about John, a 15-year-old who was deeply troubled about stealing a stick of chewing gum. Do you agree with the group who felt that John's super-sensitive conscience was the result of early childhood instruction that made him feel guilty over actions that would not ordinarily distress a child? Is it your opinion that John's guilty feelings were out of proportion to what he had done? Or do you agree with the group who felt God was truly the author of the young man's guilt because stealing is stealing and the size of the theft isn't

important? Whichever group you agree with, analyze the benefits of John's confession. Is guilt lessened or intensified by confession? See 1 John 1:9; Proverbs 28:13; Jeremiah 3:12,13.

3. How would you try to help a person who felt guilty for producing an unhealthy, defective or retarded child? What would you say to the mother whose three-year-old was crushed beneath the truck because she absent-mindedly told her daughter it was safe to cross the street? Are there some feelings of guilt for which there is no answer? Why?

4. Dr. Dobson cites the example of Walt, who became an atheist. How did guilt influence Walt's transition from believer to unbeliever? Read 2 Corinthians 11:14; 1 Peter 5:8; 2 Thessalonians 2:9 and list characteristics of Satan you discover in these verses. Is it logical to believe that Satan used guilt as a way to "devour" Walt's faith? Why?

5. Does the Bible suggest that "social acceptability" has a definite influence on a Christian's view of right and wrong? See for example Romans 12:1,2.

6. What is more dependable than your conscience when it comes to determining God's view of right? Read Psalm 119 in a modern language version and jot down all thoughts that agree with Dr. Dobson's statement "God's standards are eternal and are not open to revision or negotiation."

Living with the Conscience

1. How tender is your own conscience? If you had to compare your conscience to a flower would you say that you are (a) a violet (easily crushed); (b) a tulip (guilt

blooms for a while and then fades away); (c) a wild rose (hardy, few things bother you)?

2. First Timothy 3:9 says that deacons in the church should "keep hold of the deep truths of the faith with a clear conscience." Would you say this means: (a) being sincere; (b) being extra spiritual; (c) being humble? (Compare with other versions, especially *Phillips* and the *New English Bible.*)

3. In Acts 23:1 Paul stands before Ananias and the Jewish council and says, "I have fulfilled my duty to God in all good conscience to this day." List at least five characteristics in Paul that allowed him to make this statement. How do you match what Paul says in Acts 23:1 with his admissions in 1 Timothy 1:15 and 1 Corinthians 15:9? Do you find a clue in 2 Corinthians 12:9,10?

4. In Romans 2:15 and 2 Corinthians 1:12, Paul talks about how the conscience can bear witness and can testify. Would you say that your conscience is (a) a hostile witness; (b) a trustworthy witness; (c) an unsure witness?

5. In Romans 9:1 Paul says his conscience is confirmed in the Holy Spirit and is telling him the truth. Compare Romans 9:1 with John 16:7-14. Do you agree that when a person becomes a Christian his conscience becomes more tender and pliable? Why?

6. On page 31 Dr. Dobson lists three mental faculties and three tests to evaluate guilt. Which of these three mental faculties is most important in your opinion? Which mental faculty can cause you the most trouble when it comes to guilt? Which mental faculty do you feel Christians use the least in daily life? How does a passage like Philippians 4:8 apply?

Parental Training of the Conscience

1. Dr. Dobson writes: "The proper 'programming' of the conscience is one of the most difficult jobs associated with parenthood, and the one that requires the greatest wisdom." Compare what Dr. Dobson says with Proverbs 22:6. See also Deuteronomy 6:4-9; Ephesians 6:4. Then list as many "responsibilities for me as a parent" as you can think of.

2. Dr. Dobson writes: "When parents say they are going to withhold indoctrination from their small child, allowing him to 'decide for himself,' they are almost guaranteeing that he will 'decide' in the negative." Do you agree or disagree? What reasons does Dr. Dobson give to emphasize the importance of parental example?

3. What can you infer from the story of Eli and his sons (1 Sam. 2—4) about the importance of early training in a child's life? Finish this statement with as many specific reasons as possible: "Early training of the child (from birth) is important because . . ."

4. Dr. Dobson lists six scriptural concepts that should guide parents as they nurture their children—especially during the first seven years. As Dr. Dobson points out, the six concepts and their supporting questions are "targets" toward which the parent can gently nudge his children during their impressionable years. Educational studies (and practical experience) show that there is no more powerful teaching tool than modeling (setting an example).

What kind of example are you setting for your children in regard to Dr. Dobson's six concepts? On a scale of 1 (low) to 10 (high) rate yourself with the following inventory.

Answer each of the questions as honestly and accurately as you can. Try to stay away from a neutral, middleground approach by just marking everything with a "5." Honestly assess your attitudes and actions and mark yourself as high above 5 or as low below 5 as you feel you really are.

CONCEPT I—*Love the Lord your God with all your heart (Mark 12:30).*
Rate yourself from 1 (low) to 10 (high).

_____ 1. Does my child experience from me God's love, tenderness, forgiveness?

_____ 2. Does my child hear me talking about the Lord as I consistently include Him in my thoughts and plans?

_____ 3. Does my child see me turn to Jesus for help when I am frightened, anxious or disturbed?

_____ 4. Does my child see me reading the Bible regularly?

_____ 5. Does my child see and hear me pray each day?

_____ 6. Does my child see evidence of my faith in God as I trust Him for daily needs and direction?

_____ 7. Does my child see me demonstrate genuine appreciation and joy to God for His goodness?

_____ 8. Am I teaching my child who Jesus is and why He came to be our Saviour and Friend?

CONCEPT II—*Love your neighbor as yourself (Mark 12:31).*
Rate yourself from 1 (low) to 10 (high).

_____ 1. Does my child see and hear me trying to understand how other people feel—putting myself in their shoes?

_____ 2. Does my child see me engaging in specific acts of generosity? (Particularly, am I generous and unselfish in my relationships with my child?)

_____ 3. Does my child see me sharing my possessions and my time? (Do I share my time with my child?)

_____ 4. Does my child see me being kind in specific ways?

_____ 5. Does my child see me accepting myself as I am, not trying to be someone else? (Am I genuine and transparent?)

CONCEPT III—*Teach me to do your will, for you are my God (Ps. 143:10).*

Rate yourself from 1 (low) to 10 (high).

_____ 1. Does my child see me being obedient to authority—especially to God?

_____ 2. Do I worship in spirit and in truth—not whispering or talking but being reverent and attentive in the church services? (Am I training my child with short visits to the worship service instead of demanding that he sit still for long periods of time?)

_____ 3. Does my child hear me talk about God's love as well as God's judgment?

_____ 4. Does my child see and hear me talk positively about obeying authorities, such as policemen, employers, the pastor and others?

_____ 5. Does my child hear me ask God's forgiveness for my sins in specific terms?

CONCEPT IV—*Fear God and keep his commandments, for this is the whole duty of man (Eccles. 12:13).*

Rate yourself from 1 (low) to 10 (high).

_____ 1. Am I truthful and honest in my dealings with my child, as well as with others?

_____ 2. Does my child see me planning my Sunday activities so that they will honor God?

_____ 3. Does my child sense that I believe people are more important than things and "having things"?

_____ 4. Do I show my child that I feel our family is important by spending time together, loving one another, supporting one another?

CONCEPT V—*But the fruit of the spirit is . . . self-control (Gal. 5:22,23).*

Rate yourself from 1 (low) to 10 (high).

_____ 1. Does my child see me giving a significant percentage (at least a tithe) of my income to God?

_____ 2. Does my child see me practice self-control? For example, do I try to keep my temper in frustrating circumstances?

_____ 3. Does my child see me as self-disciplined in my attitude and approach to my work and responsibilities?

_____ 4. When I do get angry, is it valid anger that is quickly over, or do I seethe and simmer, taking it out on those around me?

_____ 5. Does my child see and hear me using Scripture in daily life—applying it, quoting it, making it important and meaningful?

CONCEPT VI—*He who humbles himself will be exalted
(Luke 14:11).*

Rate yourself from 1 (low) to 10 (high).

_____ 1. Does my child see and hear me demonstrate
appreciation—to others in the family? to friends and
acquaintances? to God?

_____ 2. Does my child hear me consistently thank God
for the many good things He brings into our lives?

_____ 3. Do I practice forgiveness of others before my
child? (Do I readily forgive my child?)

_____ 4. Does my child see me as a confident person, but
one who is not conceited?

_____ 5. Do I have genuine reverence for God and does
my child see me expressing this reverence?

How Did You Do?

As Dr. Dobson points out, parenthood is a guilt-
producing affair and most parents will tend to score
themselves too low on a personal inventory. Go back over
your answers. There may be places where you will want to
reconsider and give yourself a break.

There will be, of course, areas where you will see need
of improvement. Work on these, and keep in mind that as
you allow God to guide and direct your life, your child will
have all the better model to learn from and to imitate.

Notes

1. James Dobson, *Dare to Discipline* (Wheaton, IL: Tyndale House Publishers,
1970), pp. 172, 173.
2. Of key importance in child rearing is the kind of model (example) the parent
provides for the children.

For Further Reading

Ahlem, Lloyd H. *Do I Have to Be Me?* Ventura, CA: Regal Books, 1973. Entire book is relevant to dealing with guilt and conscience.

Dobson, James. *Dare to Discipline*. Wheaton, IL: Tyndale House Publishers, 1970. A much needed emphasis for conscientious parents.

_____ *Hide or Seek*. Old Tappan, NJ: Fleming H. Revell, 1974. Good balance for parents on building self-esteem and a sense of responsiblity.

_____ *The Strong Willed Child*. Wheaton, IL: Tyndale House Publishers, 1978. An excellent how-to book for parents of assertive boys and girls.

Haystead, Wesley. *You Can't Begin Too Soon*. Ventura, CA: Regal Books, 1974. A "must read" book for parents of young children.

Lee, Earl G. *Recycled for Living*. Ventura, CA: Regal Books, 1973. Devotional thoughts on Psalm 37 that apply to guilt and conscience.

Wright, H. Norman. *The Christian Use of Emotional Power*. Old Tappan, NJ: Fleming H. Revell, 1974. Good overall discussion with many helps on guilt and conscience.

PART II
Romantic Love

- How can the "feeling of love" become a dangerous trap?
- Why do so many couples become disillusioned shortly after the honeymoon?
- Does "love at first sight" ever occur?
- Does God select one particular person for us to marry and then guide us together?
- How can love be kept alive?

ROMANTIC LOVE: DISTORTION VERSUS THE REAL THING

It has been of concern to me that many young people grow up with a very distorted concept of romantic love. They are taught to confuse the real thing with infatuation and to idealize marriage into something it can never be. To help remedy this situation, I developed a brief true or false quiz for use in teaching groups of teenagers. But to my surprise, I found that adults did not score much higher on the quiz than their adolescent offspring.

You may want to take this quiz to measure your understanding of romance, love and marriage. A discussion of each true-false statement follows the quiz to help you discover for yourself the difference between distorted love and the real thing.

What Do You Believe About Love?

Please check the appropriate column.

		True	False
Item 1:	"Love at first sight" occurs between some people.	☐	☐
Item 2:	It is easy to distinguish real love from infatuation.	☐	☐
Item 3:	People who sincerely love each other will not fight and argue.	☐	☐
Item 4:	God selects *one* particular person for each of us to marry, and He will guide us together.	☐	☐
Item 5:	If a man and woman genuinely love each other, then hardships	☐	☐

		True	False
	and troubles will have little or no effect on their relationship.		
Item 6:	It is better to marry the wrong person than to remain single and lonely throughout life.	☐	☐
Item 7:	It is not harmful to have sexual intercourse before marriage if the couple has a meaningful relationship.	☐	☐
Item 8:	If a couple is genuinely in love, that condition is permanent—lasting a lifetime.	☐	☐
Item 9:	Short courtships (six months or less) are best.	☐	☐
Item 10:	Teenagers are more capable of genuine love than are older people.	☐	☐

Boy meets girl—hurray for love!

While there are undoubtedly some differences of opinion regarding the answers for the true-false quiz, I feel strongly about what I consider to be correct responses to each item. I believe many of the common marital hang-ups develop from a misunderstanding of these 10 issues.

Let's look at a hypothetical courtship where the meaning of love is poorly understood.

The confusion begins when boy meets girl and the entire sky lights up in romantic profusion. Smoke and fire are followed by lightning and thunder, and alas, two trembly-voiced adolescents find themselves knee-deep in true love. Adrenalin is pumped into the cardio-vascular system by the pint, and every nerve is charged with 110 volts of electricity. Then two little fellows go racing up the respective backbones and blast their exhilarated messages into each spinning head: "This is it! The search is over! You've found the perfect human being! Hooray for love!"

For our romantic young couple, it is simply too wonderful to behold. They want to be together 24 hours a day—to take walks in the rain and sit by the fire and kiss and munch and cuddle. They get all choked up just thinking about each other. And it doesn't take long for the subject of marriage to propose itself. So they set the date and reserve the chapel and contact the minister and order the flowers.

The big night arrives amidst Mother's tears and Dad's grins and jealous bridesmaids and frightened little flower girls. The candles are lit and two beautiful songs are butchered by the bride's sister. Then the vows are muttered and the rings placed on trembling fingers, and the preacher tells the groom to kiss his new wife. Then they sprint up the aisle, each flashing 32 teeth, on the way to the reception room.

Their friends and well-wishers hug and kiss the bride and roll their eyes at the groom, and eat the awful cake, and follow the instructions of the perspiring photographer. Finally the new Mr. and Mrs. run from the church in a flurry of rice and confetti and strike out on their honeymoon. So far the beautiful dream remains intact, but it is living on borrowed time.

The first night in the motel is not only less exciting than advertised—it turns into a comical disaster. She is exhausted and tense, and he is self-conscious and phony. From the beginning, sex is tinged with the threat of possible failure. Their vast expectations about the marital bed lead to disappointment and frustration and fear. Since most human beings have an almost neurotic desire to feel sexually adequate, each partner tends to blame his mate for their orgasmic problems, which eventually adds a note of anger and resentment to their relationship.

About three o'clock on the second afternoon, the new husband gives 10 minutes thought to the fateful question, "Have I made an enormous mistake?" His silence increases her anxieties, and the seeds of disenchantment are born. Each partner has far too much time to think about the consequences of this new relationship, and they both begin to feel trapped.

Their initial argument is a silly thing. They struggle momentarily over how much money to spend for dinner on the third night of the honeymoon. She wants to go someplace romantic to charge up the atmosphere, and he wants to eat with Ronald McDonald. The flare-up only lasts a few moments and is followed by apologies, but some harsh words have been exchanged which took the keen edge off the beautiful dream. They will soon learn to hurt each other more effectively.

Somehow, they make it through the six-day trip and drive home to set up housekeeping together. Then the world starts to splinter and disintegrate before their eyes. The next fight is bigger and better than the first; he leaves home for two hours and she calls her mother.

Throughout the first year, they will be engaged in an enormous contest of wills, each vying for power and leadership. And in the midst of this tug-of-war, she staggers out of the obstetrician's office with the words ringing in her ears, "I have some good news for you, Mrs. Jones!" If there is anything on earth Mrs. Jones doesn't need at that time, it is "good news" from an obstetrician.

From there to the final conflict, we see two disappointed, confused and deeply hurt young people, wondering how it all came about. We also see a little tow-headed lad who will never enjoy the benefits of a stable home. He'll be raised by his mother and will always wonder, "Why doesn't Dad live here anymore?"

The picture I have painted does not reflect every young marriage, obviously, but it is representative of far too many of them. The divorce rate is higher in America than in any other civilized nation in the world, and it is rising. In the case of our disillusioned young couple, what happened to their romantic dream? How did the relationship that began with such enthusiasm turn so quickly into hatred and hostility? They could not possibly have been more enamored with each other at the beginning, but their "happiness" blew up in their startled faces. Why didn't it last? How can others avoid the same unpleasant surprise?

First we need to understand the true meaning of romantic love. Perhaps the answers to our quiz will help accomplish that objective.

BELIEFS ABOUT LOVE

Item 1: "Love at first sight" occurs between some people—true or false?

Though some readers will disagree with me, love at

first sight is a physical and emotional impossibility. Why? Because love is not simply a feeling of romantic excitement; it goes beyond intense sexual attraction; it exceeds the thrill at having "captured" a highly desirable social prize. These are emotions that are unleashed at first sight, but they *do not constitute love*. I wish the whole world knew that fact. These temporary feelings differ from love in that they place the spotlight on the one experiencing them. "What is happening to *Me*? This is the most fantastic thing *I've* ever been through! *I* think *I* am in love!"

You see, these emotions are selfish in the sense that they are motivated by our own gratification. They have little to do with the new lover. Such a person has not fallen in love with another person; *he has fallen in love with love!* And there is an enormous difference between the two.

The popular songs in the world of teenage music reveal a vast ignorance of the meaning of love. One immortal number asserts, "Before the dance was through, I knew I was in luv with yew." I wonder if the crooner will be quite so confident tomorrow morning. Another confesses, "I didn't know just what to do, so I whispered 'I luv yew!' " That one really gets to me. The idea of basing a lifetime commitment on sheer confusion seems a bit shaky, at best.

The Partridge Family recorded a song which also betrays a lack of understanding of real love; it said, "I woke up in love today 'cause I went to sleep with you on my mind." You see, love in this sense is nothing more than a frame of mind—it's just about that permanent. Finally, a rock group of the 60s called *The Doors* takes the prize for the most ignorant musical number of the century; it was called, "Hello, I love you, won't you tell me your name!"

Did you know that the idea of marriage based on romantic affection is a very recent development in human affairs? Prior to A.D. 1200, weddings were arranged by the families of the bride and groom, and it never occurred to anyone that they were supposed to "fall in love." In fact, the concept of romantic love was actually popularized by William Shakespeare. There are times when I wish the old Englishman was here to help us straighten out the mess that he initiated.

Real love, in contrast to popular notions, is an expression of the deepest appreciation for another human being; it is an intense awareness of his or her needs and longings for the past, present and future. It is unselfish and giving and caring. And believe me these are not attitudes one "falls" into at first sight, as though he were tumbling into a ditch.

I have developed a lifelong love for my wife, but it was not something I fell into. I *grew* into it, and that process took time. I had to know her before I could appreciate the depth and stability of her character—to become acquainted with the nuances of her personality, which I now cherish. The familiarity from which love has blossomed simply could not be generated on "Some enchanted evening . . . across a crowded room." One cannot love an unknown object, regardless of how attractive or sexy or nubile it is!

Item 2: It is easy to distinguish real love from infatuation—true or false?

The answer is, again, false. That wild ride at the start of a romantic adventure bears all the earmarks of a lifetime trip. Just try to tell a starry-eyed 16-year-old dreamer that he is not really in love—that he's merely infatuated. He'll whip out his guitar and sing you a song. "Young luv, true luv. Filled with real emo-shun. Young luv, true luv. Filled with true devoshun!" He knows what he feels, and he feels great. But he'd better enjoy the roller-coaster ride while it lasts, because it has a predictable end point.

I must stress this fact with the greatest emphasis: The exhilaration of infatuation is *never* a permanent condition. Period! If you expect to live on the top of that mountain, year after year, you can forget it! Emotions swing from high to low to high in cyclical rhythm, and since romantic excitement is an emotion, it too will certainly oscillate. If the thrill of sexual encounter is identified as genuine love, then disillusionment and disappointment are already knocking at the door.

How many vulnerable young couples "fall in love with love" on the first date—and lock themselves into marriage before the natural swing of their emotions has even progressed through the first dip? They then wake up one morning without that neat feeling and conclude that love has died. In reality, it was never there in the first place. They were fooled by an emotional "high."

I was trying to explain this up-and-down characteristic of our psychological nature to a group of 100 young married couples to whom I was speaking. During the discussion period, someone asked a young man in the group why he got married so young, and he replied, " 'Cause I didn't know 'bout that wiggly line until it was too late!" Alas, 'tis true. That wiggly line has trapped more than one young romanticist.

The "wiggly line" is manipulated up and down by the circumstances of life. Even when a man and woman love each other deeply and genuinely, they will find themselves supercharged on one occasion and emotionally bland on another! You see, their love is not defined by the highs and lows, but is dependent *on a commitment of their will*! Stability comes from this irrepressible determination to make a success of marriage, and to keep the flame aglow *regardless of the circumstances*.

Unfortunately, not everyone agrees with the divinely inspired concept of permanent marriage. We have heard the noted anthropologist, Dr. Margaret Mead, advocate trial marriage for the young; we have been propagandized to accept communal marriage and contract marriage and cohabitation. Even our music has reflected our aimless groping for an innovative relationship between men and women.

One such idea is that romantic love can only survive in the *absence* of permanent commitment. Singer Glen Campbell translated this thought into music in his popular song entitled "Gentle on My Mind." Paraphrasing the lyrics, he said it was not the ink-stained signatures dried on some marriage certificate that kept his bedroll stashed behind the couch in his lover's home; it was knowing that he could get up and leave her anytime he wished—that she had no hooks into his hide. It was the freedom to abandon her that kept her "gentle on [his] mind."

What a ridiculous notion to think a woman exists who could let her lover come and go with no feelings of loss, rejection, or abandonment. How ignorant it is of the power of love (and sex) to make us "one flesh," inevitably ripping and tearing that flesh at the time of separation.

And, of course, Brother Campbell's song said nothing about the little children who are born from such a relationship, each one wondering if Daddy will be there tomorrow morning, if he will help them pay their bills, or if he'll be out by a railroad track somewhere sipping coffee from a tin can and thinking the good thoughts in the backroads of his mind. Can't you see his little woman standing with her children in the front doorway, waving a hanky and calling, "Good-bye, Dear. Drop in when you can"?

Let's return to the question before us: if genuine love is rooted in a commitment of the will, how can one know when it arrives? How can it be distinguished from temporary infatuation? How can the feeling be interpreted if it is unreliable and inconstant?

There is only one answer to those questions: *it takes time.* The best advice I can give a couple contemplating marriage (or any other important decision) is this: make *no* important, life-shaping decisions quickly or impulsively, and when in doubt, stall for time. That's not a bad suggestion for all of us to apply.

Item 3: People who sincerely love each other will not fight and argue—true or false?

I doubt if this third item actually requires an answer. Some marital conflict is as inevitable as the sunrise, even in loving marriages. There is a difference, however, between healthy and unhealthy combat, depending on the way the disagreement is handled. In an unstable marriage, anger is usually hurled directly at the partner. Hostile, person-centered "you messages" strike at the heart of one's self-worth and produce intensive internal upheaval:

"You never do anything right!"

"Why did I ever marry you?"

"How can you be so stupid (or unreasonable or unfair)?"

"You are getting more like your mother every day."

The wounded partner often responds in like manner, hurling back every unkind and hateful remark he or she can concoct, punctuated with tears and profanity. The avowed purpose of this kind of in-fighting is to hurt, and it does. The cutting words will never be forgotten, even though uttered in a moment of irrational anger. Such combat is not only unhealthy; it is vicious and corrosive. It erodes the marriage relationship, and can easily destroy it.

Healthy conflict, on the other hand, remains focused on the issue around which the disagreement began. Issue centered, "I" messages let your partner know what is wrong, but that he or she is not the main target:

"I'm worried about all these bills."

"I get upset when I don't know you'll be late for dinner."

"I was embarrassed by what you said at the party last night—I felt foolish."

Any area of struggle—worry, anger, embarrassment—can be emotional and tense, but it can be much less damaging to the egos of both spouses if they will focus on the basic disagreement and try to resolve it together. A healthy couple can work through problems by compromise and negotiation. There will still be pain and hurt, but a husband and wife will have fewer imbedded barbs to pluck out the following morning.

The ability to fight *properly* may be the most important

concept to be learned by newlyweds. Those who never comprehend the technique are usually left with two alternatives: (1) turn the anger and resentment inward in silence, where it will fester and accumulate through the years, or (2) blast away at the personhood of one's mate. The divorce courts are well represented by couples in both categories.[1]

Item 4: God selects one particular person for each of us to marry, and He will guide us together—true or false?

A young man whom I was counseling once told me that he awoke in the middle of the night with the strong impression that God wanted him to marry a young lady whom he had only dated casually a few times. They were not even going together at that moment and hardly knew each other. The next morning he called her and relayed the message which God had supposedly sent him during the night. The girl figured she shouldn't argue with God, and she accepted the proposal. They have now been married for seven years and have struggled for survival since their wedding day!

Anyone who believes that God guarantees a successful marriage to every Christian is in for a shock. This is not to say that He is disinterested in the choice of a mate, or that He will not answer a specific request for guidance on this all-important decision. Certainly, His will should be sought in such a critical matter, and I consulted Him repeatedly before proposing to my wife.

However, I do not believe that God performs a routine matchmaking service for everyone who worships Him. He has given us judgment, common sense and discretionary powers, and He expects us to exercise these abilities in matters matrimonial. Those who believe otherwise are likely to enter marriage glibly, thinking, "God would have stopped us if He didn't approve." To such confident people I can only say, "Lotsa luck."

Item 5: If a man and woman genuinely love each other, then hardships and troubles will have little or no effect on their relationship—true or false?

Another common misconception about the meaning of "true love" is that it inevitably stands like the rock of Gibraltar against the storms of life. Many people apparently believe that love is destined to conquer all. The Beatles endorsed this notion with their song, "All we need is love, love, love is all we need." Unfortunately, we need a bit more.

As I mentioned before, I serve on the Attending Staff for Children's Hospital of Los Angeles. We see numerous genetic and metabolic problems throughout the year, most of which involve mental retardation in our young patients. The emotional impact of such a diagnosis on the families involved is sometimes devastating. Even in stable, loving marriages, the guilt and disappointment of having produced a "broken" child often drives a wedge of isolation between the distressed mother and father. In a similar manner, the fiber of love can be weakened by financial hardships, disease, business setbacks or prolonged separation. In short, we must conclude that love is vulnerable to pain and trauma, and often wobbles when assaulted by life.

Item 6: It is better to marry the wrong person than to remain single and lonely throughout life—true or false?

Again, the answer is false. Generally speaking, it is less painful to be searching for an end to loneliness than to be embroiled in the emotional combat of a sour marriage. Yet the threat of being an "old maid" (a term I detest) causes many girls to grab the first train that rambles down the marital track. And too often, it offers a one-way ticket to disaster.

The fear of never finding a mate can cause a single person to ignore his better judgment and compromise his own standards. A young woman, particularly, may argue with herself in this manner: "John isn't a Christian, but maybe I can influence him after we're married. He drinks too much, but that's probably because he's young and carefree. And we don't have much in common, but I'm sure we'll learn to love each other more as time passes. Besides, what could be worse than living alone?"

This kind of rationalization is based on a desperate hope for a matrimonial miracle, but storybook endings are uncommon events in everyday life. When one plunges into marriage despite the obvious warning flags, he is gambling with the remaining years of his earthly existence.

For those readers who are single today, *please* believe me when I say that a bad marriage is among the most miserable experiences on earth! It is filled with rejection and hurt feelings and hatred and screaming and broken children and sleepless nights. Certainly, a solitary walk as a single person can be a meaningful and fulfilling life; at least, it does not involve "a house divided against itself."

Item 7: It is not harmful to have sexual intercourse before marriage, if the couple has a meaningful relationship—true or false?

This item represents *the* most dangerous of the popular misconceptions about romantic love, not only for individuals but for our future as a nation. During the past 15 years we have witnessed the tragic disintegration of our sexual mores and traditional concepts of morality. Responding to a steady onslaught by the entertainment industry and by the media, our people have begun to believe that premarital intercourse is a noble experience, extramarital encounters are healthy, homosexuality is acceptable, and bisexuality is even better. These views—labeled as "the new morality"—reflect the sexual stupidity of the age in which we live, yet they are believed and applied by millions of American citizens.

As I stated in Part I, a recent study of college students revealed that 25 percent of them have shared bedrooms with a member of the opposite sex for at least three months. According to *Life Styles and Campus Communities,* 66 percent of college students reportedly believe premarital intercourse is acceptable between any two people who consent or "when a couple has dated some and care a lot about each other."

I have never considered myself to be a prophet of doom, but I am admittedly alarmed by statistical evidence of this nature. I view these trends with fear and trepidation, seeing in them the potential death of our society and our way of life.

Mankind has known intuitively for at least 50 centuries that indiscriminate sexual activity represents both an individual and a corporate threat to survival. And history bears it out. Anthropologist J.D. Unwin conducted an exhaustive study of the 88 civilizations which have existed in the history of the world. Each culture has reflected a similar life cycle, beginning with a strict code of sexual conduct and ending with the demand for complete "freedom" to express individual passion. Unwin reports that *every* society which extended sexual permissiveness to its people was soon to perish. There have been no exceptions.[2]

Why do you suppose the reproductive urge within us is so relevant to cultural survival? It is because the energy which holds a people together is sexual in nature! The physical attraction between men and women causes them to establish a family and invest themselves in its development. It encourages them to work and save and toil to insure the survival of their families. Their sexual energy provides the impetus for the raising of healthy children and for the transfer of values from one generation to the next.

Sexual drives urge a man to work when he would rather play. They cause a woman to save when she would rather spend. In short, the sexual aspect of our nature—when released exclusively within the family—produces stability and responsibility that would not otherwise occur. When a nation is composed of millions of devoted, responsible family units, the entire society is stable, responsible and resilient.

If sexual energy within the family is the key to a healthy society, then its release outside those boundaries is potentially catastrophic. The very force that binds a people together then becomes the agent for its own destruction.

Perhaps this point can be illustrated by an analogy between sexual energy in the nuclear family and physical energy in the nucleus of a tiny atom. Electrons, neutrons and protons are held in delicate balance by an electrical force within each atom. But when that atom and its neighbors are split in nuclear fission (such as in an atomic bomb), the energy which had provided the internal stability is then released with unbelievable power and destruction. There is ample reason to believe that this comparison between the atom and the family is more than incidental.

Who can deny that a society is seriously weakened when the intense sexual urge between men and women becomes an instrument for suspicion and intrigue within millions of individual families:

• when a woman never knows what her husband is doing when away from home

• when a husband can't trust his wife in his absence

• when half of the brides are pregnant at the altar

• when both newlyweds have slept with numerous partners, losing the exclusive wonder of the marital bed

• when everyone is doing his own thing, particularly that which brings him immediate sensual gratification!

Unfortunately, the most devastated victim of an immoral society of this nature is the vulnerable child who hears his parents scream and argue. Their tensions and frustrations spill over into his world, and the instability of his home leaves its ugly scars on his young mind. Then he watches his parents separate in anger, and he says goodbye to the father he needs and loves.

Or perhaps we should speak of the thousands of babies born to unmarried teenage mothers each year—

many of whom will never know the meaning of a warm, nurturing home. Or maybe we should discuss the rampant scourge of venereal disease which has reached epidemic proportions among America's youth.

Illegitimate births, heartbreak, shattered personalities, abortions, disease, even death—this is the true vomitus of the sexual revolution, and I am tired of hearing it romanticized and glorified. God has clearly forbidden irresponsible sexual behavior, not to deprive us of fun and pleasure, but to spare us the disastrous consequences of this festering way of life. Those individuals and those nations choosing to defy His commandments on this issue will pay a dear price for their folly.

Item 8: If a couple is genuinely in love, that condition is permanent—lasting a lifetime—true or false?

Love, even genuine love, is a fragile thing. It must be maintained and protected if it is to survive. Love can perish when a husband works seven days a week, when there is no time for romantic activity, when he and his wife forget how to talk to each other.

The keen edge in a loving relationship may be dulled through the routine pressures of living, as I experienced during the early days of my marriage to Shirley. I was working full time and trying to finish my doctorate at the University of Southern California. My wife was teaching school and maintaining our small home. I remember clearly the evening that I realized what this busy life was doing to our relationship. We still loved each other, but it had been too long since we had felt a spirit of warmth and closeness. My textbooks were pushed aside that night and we went for a long walk. The following semester I carried a very light load in school and postponed my academic goals so as to preserve that which I valued more highly.

Where does your marriage rank on your hierarchy of values? Does it get the leftovers and scraps from your busy schedule or is it something of great worth to be preserved and supported? It can die if left untended.

Item 9: Short courtships (six months or less) are best—true or false?

The answer to this question is incorporated in the reply to the second item regarding infatuation. Short courtships require impulsive decisions about lifetime commitments, and that is risky business, at best.

Item 10: Teenagers are more capable of genuine love than are older people—true or false?

If this item were true, then we would be hard pressed to explain why half the teenage marriages end in divorce in the first five years. To the contrary, the kind of love I have been describing—unselfish, giving, caring commitment—requires a sizeable dose of maturity to make it work. And maturity is a partial thing in most teenagers. Adolescent romance is an exciting part of growing up, but it seldom meets the criteria for the deeper relationships of which successful marriages are composed.

I AM COMMITTED TO YOU

All 10 items on this brief questionnaire are false, for

they represent the 10 most common misconceptions about the meaning of romantic love. Sometimes I wish the test could be used as a basis for issuing marriage licenses: those scoring 9 or 10 would qualify with honor; those getting 5-8 items right would be required to wait an extra 6 months before marriage; those confused dreamers answering 4 or less items correctly would be recommended for permanent celibacy! (Seriously, what we probably need is a cram-course for everyone contemplating wedding bells.)

In conclusion, I want to share the words I wrote to my wife on an anniversary card on our eighth anniversary. What I said to her may not be expressed in the way you would communicate with your mate. I do hope, however, that my words illustrate the "genuine, uncompromising love" I have been describing:

To My Darlin' Little Wife, Shirley
on the occasion of our Eighth Anniversary

I'm sure you remember the many, many occasions during our eight years of marriage when the tide of love and affection soared high above the crest—times when our feeling for each other was almost limitless. This kind of intense emotion can't be brought about voluntarily, but it often accompanies a time of particular happiness. We felt it when I was offered my first professional position. We felt it when the world's most precious child came home from the maternity ward of Huntington Hospital. We felt it when the University of Southern California chose to award a doctoral degree to me. But emotions are strange! We felt the same closeness when the opposite kind of event took place; when threat and potential disaster entered our lives. We felt an intense closeness when a medical problem threatened to postpone our marriage plans. We felt it when you were hospitalized last year. I felt it intensely when I knelt over your unconscious form after a grinding automobile accident.

I'm trying to say this: both happiness and threat bring that overwhelming appreciation and affection for a person's beloved sweetheart. But the fact is, most of life is made up of neither disaster nor unusual hilarity. Rather, it is composed of the routine, calm, everyday events in which we participate. And during these times, I enjoy the quiet, serene love that actually surpasses the effervescent display, in many ways. It is not as exuberant, perhaps, but it runs deep and solid. I find myself firmly in that kind of love on this Eighth Anniversary. Today I feel the steady and quiet affection that comes from a devoted heart. I am committed to you and your happiness, now more than I've ever been. I want to remain your "sweetheart."

When events throw us together emotionally, we will enjoy the thrill and romantic excitement. But during life's routine, like today, my love stands undiminished. Happy Anniversary to my wonderful wife.

Jim

The key phrase in my note to Shirley is, "I am committed to you." My love for my wife is not blown back and forth by the winds of change, by circumstances and environmental influences. Even though my fickle emotions jump from one extreme to another, my commitment remains solidly anchored. I have chosen to love my wife, and that choice is sustained by an uncompromising will.

The essential investment of commitment is sorely missing in so many modern marriages. I love you, they seem to say, as long as I feel attracted to you—or as long as someone else doesn't look better—or as long as it is to my advantage to continue the relationship. Sooner or later, this unanchored love will certainly vaporize.

"For better or worse, for richer for poorer, in sickness and in health, to love, and to cherish, till death us do part. . . ."

That familiar pledge from the past still offers the most solid foundation upon which to build a marriage, for therein lies the real meaning of genuine romantic love.

LEARNING-DISCUSSION IDEAS

Are you reading this book alone? With your spouse? With a study group? Whatever your situation, the following questions, agree/disagree statements, life-situations and Bible study ideas will help you work with Dr. Dobson's views as he discusses 10 common misconceptions about romance, love, marriage. Equip yourself with a notebook, Bible and pencil and you are ready to work with these learning-discussion ideas.

Item 1: "Love at first sight" occurs between some people—true or false?

1. Do you agree or disagree with Dr. Dobson's view

that "love at first sight" is physically and emotionally impossible? Can the kind of relationship described in Philippians 2:2 exist in "love at first sight"? Why? Why not?

2. Do you agree with Dr. Dobson that popular songs help distort a person's concept of love? What about films? TV? Magazine fiction? How can you tell the difference between "falling in love with love" and developing a genuine love relationship with someone? What does a passage like Colossians 3:12-15 have to do with "true love" in a marriage?

3. Is selfishness involved in "love at first sight"? Why? Why not? For ideas on love and selfishness read Philippians 2:2-4.

4. Read the last two paragraphs in Dr. Dobson's discussion of "love at first sight" (p. 57, paragraph beginning, "Real love . . . "). List reasons the words "time" and "grow" are important to real love. Read different versions of 1 Corinthians 13:4-7 and note words and phrases that you feel are related to the idea of taking time to grow into love.

Item 2: It is easy to distinguish real love from infatuation—true or false?

1. Do you agree or disagree with Dr. Dobson that: "The exhilaration of infatuation is *never* a permanent condition"?

Discussion ideas: Is any relationship immune from ups and downs? Is any situation permanent? Can anyone truthfully say, "I won't change"? Read Malachi 3:6 and Hebrews 13:8. How can God's changelessness strengthen and give stability to a human relationship? (See Ps. 33:11.)

2. Does the following statement by Dr. Dobson strike you as (1) unromantic; (2) puzzling; (3) false; (4) a solid base for marriage? "Stability [in marriage] comes from this irrepressible determination to make a success of marriage, and to keep the flame aglow *regardless of the circumstances.*" Explain your response. How do Romans 15:5 and 1 Thessalonians 5:11 compare with the statement?

3. According to Dr. Dobson what is the necessary ingredient that must be added before you can really determine whether a person is experiencing infatuation or genuine love? Proverbs 19:2 talks about the wisdom of taking time to think through any important step when it says: "It is not good . . . to be hasty and miss the way." How can this apply to evaluating infatuation and real love? What are the unknowns?

Item 3: People who sincerely love each other will not fight and argue—true or false?

1. "Some marital conflict is inevitable," says Dr. Dobson. What is the key to keeping the combat zone healthy? Read Dr. Dobson's comments in the two paragraphs following Item 3. For additional ideas read Proverbs 15:1,18; 17:14; Ephesians 4:26,27.

2. True or false? Can a married couple argue and still obey the teaching in Ephesians 4:31?

3. Discuss the difference between being angry at your spouse and being angry or hurt by the issue or the problem. Is it always possible to keep the two separated? What guides for constructive conflict can you find in Galatians 5:15; 1 Peter 4:8 and James 5:16. Read the verses in as many versions as possible. List three key ideas.

4. If you are in a study group situation, ask volunteers to roleplay an argument that demonstrates the principle: "healthy conflict . . . remains focused on the issue around which the disagreement began." For each roleplay choose from the following three issues:

"I'm worried about all these bills."

"I get upset when I don't know you'll be late for dinner."

"I was embarrassed by what you said at the party last night—I felt foolish."

After each roleplay argument take a few minutes for the entire group to evaluate: did the argument stay on the issue, or did it become personal?

Item 4: God selects one particular person for each of us to marry and He will guide us together—true or false?

1 How does God offer help for choosing a marriage partner? Before you decide on your answer read Jeremiah 33:3; 1 Chronicles 16:11; Philippians 4:6; James 1:5-8. Is the help described in these verses general or specific?

2. What does 2 Corinthians 6:14 reveal about God's will for a Christian's choice of a marriage partner? In your opinion, what is more important? That a prospective mate be a Christian or that he or she be mature, kind, patient, etc.? Give reasons for your answer.

3. Dr. Dobson says, "Anyone who believes that God guarantees a successful marriage to every Christian is in for a shock." What do you feel he means by this statement? Do you agree or disagree?

Item 5: If a man and woman genuinely love each other, then hardships and troubles will have little or no effect on their relationship—true or false?

1. Do you agree or disagree with Dr. Dobson's belief that the emotional impact of trouble can be devastating even in a stable loving marriage? Why? Give real life evidence (that you have observed) to support your view.

2. What resources do Christian couples have to help them face trouble and work out problems? Which of the following Bible passages would give you the most encouragement in times of trouble? Joshua 1:9; Psalm 3; Colossians 2:6,7; 1 Peter 5:8-11.

3. Dr. Dobson speaks of the "wedge of isolation" that trouble can drive between a distressed husband and wife (mother and father). Identify at least three principles given in 1 John 3:18; 4:7; 1 Thessalonians 5:11; Philippians 2:4 that can help marriage partners reach out to each other in troubled times and avoid the "wedge of isolation."

4. List ways to protect love from "the pain and trauma" of trouble. From the following Scripture portions choose ways to protect and strengthen love, even when things are rough: Galatians 6:2; Romans 12:15; 1 Peter 3:8,9. Which of these ways do you need to work on in your marriage this week? Which will require the most change in you?

Item 6: It is better to marry the wrong person than to remain single and lonely throughout life—true or false?

1. Dr. Dobson says, "It is [usually] less painful to be searching for an end to loneliness than to be embroiled in

the emotional combat of a sour marriage." Do you agree or disagree? Why?

2. Do statements made in Proverbs 15:17; 17:1 and Ecclesiastes 4:6 favor loneliness or marriage to a "wrong person"?

3. List five constructive suggestions for ways a man can combat loneliness. Also list five specific ways a lonely woman can fill her life with meaningful activities. List your ideas under such headings as: Personal Enrichment; Caring About Others; Discovering New Things; Spiritual Growth.

4. In 1 Corinthians 7:8,9 the apostle Paul encourages Christians to remain single, if possible. What are some spiritual advantages unmarried people enjoy?

Item 7: It is not harmful to have sexual intercourse before marriage, if the couple has a meaningful relationship—true or false?

1. Discuss specific ways the entertainment industry and other media communicate the view that premarital intercourse is acceptable between any two people who consent.

2. Dr. Dobson cites anthropological studies showing how all civilizations that move from a strict code for sexual conduct to wide open "sexual freedom" end in disaster.

How can a society enforce a strict code of sexual conduct and still preserve the freedom of the individual?

3. Dr. Dobson writes: "When a nation is composed of millions of devoted, responsible family units, the entire society is stable, responsible and resilient." Do you agree or disagree? How does our society match up to this?

4. Keep in mind that fornication is defined as sexual intercourse on the part of unmarried persons. Then, using the following Bible references as resources write a brief paragraph explaining the biblical view of premarital intercourse. See: Mark 7:21; 1 Corinthians 6:13-20; Galatians 5:19-21; Ephesians 5:13.

Item 8: If a couple is genuinely in love, that condition is permanent—lasting a lifetime—true or false?

1. Dr. Dobson states: "Love, even genuine love, is a fragile thing. It must be maintained and protected if it is to survive." If you are married identify and list three to five things you have experienced in your marriage that put a strain on your loving feelings. List three to five experiences that definitely strengthened your love for your spouse. (If you are engaged, or dating on a steady basis, try talking together about this and identifying problems that could put a strain on a love relationship within marriage.)

2. Read 1 Corinthians 13:4-7 in as many versions as possible. From this Bible passage write a prescription for strengthening love.

3. Quickly go through your activities of the past few days. Based on what you did, decide where your marriage rates on your value scale. Is it getting scraps and leftovers from your busy schedule? Or are you treating your marriage as something of great worth? Make a "to do" list for the next three days. Take into account your work load, demand of your family, etc. Does your "to do" list include times with your spouse? Will you give these times number 1 priority? Why? Why not?

Item 9: Short courtships (six months or less) are best—true or false?

1. To think through the validity of this statement use the questions, statements and discussion ideas for Item 2.

2. Dr. Dobson believes that six months is far too short a time for courtship. In your opinion, how long should a courtship last? How long did yours last? Could you have used more time to find out more about each other?

3. Is it possible for a courtship to be *too long*? Why?

4. If you are married, what did you learn about the personality and character of your mate after becoming husband and wife?

Item 10: Teenagers are more capable of genuine love than older people—true or false?

1. Genuine love demands caring for the other person, commitment to the other person, giving unselfishly of self. Why can these be difficult demands for teenagers to meet?

2. Compare Dr. Dobson's anniversary note to his wife with Ephesians 5:28-33. What does the Ephesians Scripture passage have to say about being commmitted to one another? When you are committed to someone else, how do you feel? What do you say and do?

3. Read Genesis 2:24 and discuss: what does it mean to become one flesh? List specific ways you and your spouse are one flesh.

Notes

1. For more information on how to handle conflict in a healthy way. read Lloyd H. Ahlem. *How to Cope* (Ventura. CA: Regal Books. 1978); also David Augsburger, *Caring Enough to Confront*, rev. ed. (Ventura. CA: Regal Books. 1980).

2. J.D. Unwin, *Sexual Regulations and Cultural Behavior.* Copyright 1969 by Frank M. Darrow, P.O. Box 305, Trona, California 93562.

For Further Reading

Ahlem, Lloyd H. *How to Cope.* Ventura, CA: Regal Books, 1978. Insights from Scripture combined with solid psychological principles provide practical guidance for handling the conflicts, crises and changes of everyday living.

Augsburger, David. *Caring Enough to Confront.* rev. ed. Ventura, CA: Regal Books, 1980. A life-style for Christians who care enough to confront others when conflicts arise.

Dobson, James. *Straight Talk to Men and Their Wives.* Waco, TX: Word, Inc., 1980.

Lee, Mark. *Creative Christian Marriage.* Ventura, CA: Regal Books, 1977. Covers the basic issues faced in marriage, from achieving mutual interests to solving sexual tensions to mending broken communication lines.

Narramore, Clyde M. *How to Succeed in Family Living.* Ventura, CA: Regal Books, 1968. A noted Christian psychologist emphasizes biblical principles of love and discipline for healthy, happy homes.

Peterson, J. Allen, ed. *Two Become One.* Wheaton, IL. Tyndale House Publishers, 1975. Excellent Bible study guide.

Shedd, Charlie. *Letters to Karen.* Nashville: Abingdon Press, 1975.

_____ *Letters to Phillip.* Nashville: Abingdon Press, 1969.

Small, Dwight. *After You've Said I Do.* Old Tappan, NJ: Fleming H. Revell Company, 1968. A comprehensive study of communication in marriage—ways to strengthen the marriage relationship.

_____ *Design for a Christian Marriage.* Old Tappan, NJ: Fleming H. Revell Company, 1959.

Wright, H. Norman. *Communication: Key to Your Marriage.* Ventura, CA: Regal Books, 1974. How to develop communication skills to cope with marital conflicts, plus practical principles for building a partner's self-esteem, handling anger and avoiding anxiety.

_____ *The Pillars of Marriage.* Ventura, CA: Regal Books, 1979. A discussion of eight "pillars" of a strong marriage: developing goals, fulfilling expectations, determining needs, handling change and crisis, making decisions, resolving conflicts, praying, forgiving.

PART III
Anger

- Is all "anger" sinful?
- How can strong negative feelings be handled without violating scriptural principles and without repressing them into the unconscious mind?
- Is it possible for the Christian to live without feelings of irritation or hostility?
- Does being morally "right" in a particular instance justify an attitude of resentment and antagonism?
- What is the "flight or fight" mechanism, and how does it relate to biblical understandings?

CONFLICT IN A FLORAL SHOP

As an impetuous young student in college, I had perfected the art of verbal combat to a high level of proficiency. I took pride in my ability to "put down" an opponent, particularly those whom I perceived as being unfair or disrespectful to me or my friends. It is a skill which I recall with some embarrassment today, although the exchange of insults and verbal abuse is not uncharacteristic of young people between 18 and 22 years of age.

After graduating from college and getting married, however, I began to be aware that God disapproved of the way I handled human conflict. "A soft answer turneth away wrath," I read in Proverbs, and the same theme was inescapable throughout the teachings of Jesus. This was plainly an area wherein the Lord expected me to bring my behavior into harmony with His Word. Yet, the bad habits of childhood are not easily broken.

It seems as though divine providence allowed a series of offensive people to cross my path during that period, each one teaching me a little more about self-control and tolerance. Every time I failed to represent the Christian love I professed, the Holy Spirit seemed to rebuke me in the days that followed. There were many "tests" involved in this learning experience, but the final examination occurred about three years later.

I had decided to surprise my wife with a corsage on Easter Sunday morning, being a firm believer in marital "flower power." The local florist took my order and promised that an orchid would be ready after five o'clock Saturday night. All week long I harbored this noble deed in my generous heart, smiling to myself and anticipating the moment of truth after breakfast the following Sunday.

When Saturday afternoon rolled around, I found a phony excuse to leave in the car for a few minutes, and drove to the florist to retrieve the secret package. The shop was crowded with customers and the lady behind the counter was obviously overworked and stressed. My first mistake, I suppose, was in not perceiving her tension soon enough, or the beads of sweat which ringed her upper lip. I patiently waited my turn and watched each patron carry his order past me and out the door. When I finally reached the counter and gave my name, the saleslady shuffled through a stack of tickets, and then said matter-of-factly, "We're not going to be able to fill your order. You'll just have to get your flowers somewhere else."

She did not offer a reason or apologize for the error. Her voice had a definite take-it-or-leave-it sound which I found irritating. She stood, hands on hips, glaring at me as though *I* had somehow caused the mistake.

At first I was puzzled, and then I asked, "Why did you accept my order if you were unable to prepare it? I could have gone somewhere else, but now it is too late to buy a corsage at another shop."

I remember distinctly that my response was very controlled under the circumstances, although my displeasure was no doubt apparent. My brief question had no sooner been uttered than a curtain swung open at the rear of the building and a red-faced man burst into the shop. He stormed toward me and pressed his chest against mine. I have no idea how big he was; I only know that I'm six-foot-two and weigh 190 pounds, yet, my eyes focused somewhere between his pulsating Adam's apple and his quivering chin. It was immediately apparent that Goliath was not merely upset—he was livid with rage! He curled his lip upward and shook his clenched fist in the vicinity of my jaw.

For the next two minutes or so, he unloaded the most violent verbal attack I had ever sustained. He used every curse word I knew and then taught me a few I hadn't even heard in the Army. Then, after questioning my heritage, he announced his intention of throwing a certain portion of my anatomy out the front door.

It is difficult to describe the emotional shock of that moment. It was a conflict I neither sought nor anticipated. Suddenly, without warning, I had tripped a spring that must have been winding tighter and tighter throughout that hectic day (or year). The next move was clearly mine. Silence fell on the shop as a half-dozen customers gasped and awaited my response.

The toughest part of the encounter involved the instantaneous conflict between what my impulses dictated and what God had been trying to teach me. In a matter of two or three seconds, it seemed as though the Lord said to me, "Are you going to obey Me, or not?"

I muttered some kind of defensive reply, and then did the most difficult thing I had ever been required to do: I turned on my heels and walked from the shop. To the customers, I probably appeared cowardly—especially in view of the size of my adversary. Or, perhaps they assumed I could think of no appropriate reply. All of these agitating thoughts reverberated through my head as I walked to my car.

Did I go home in triumph at having done what God

wanted of me? Certainly not immediately. Hot blood pulsed through my neck and ears, and adrenalin surged through my veins. My immediate response was to do something primitive—like heave a brick through the window where a bouquet of roses sat. Gradually, however, my physiological state returned to normal and I looked back on my restraint with some satisfaction.

The kind of frustration I experienced in the floral shop, whether it be called anger or some related emotion, is of importance to others trying to live the Christian life. I'm not the only one who has had to learn how to control his tongue and the tumultuous undercurrents which often propel it. But what *does* God expect of us in this area of our lives? Does He want us to be bland, colorless individuals who have no feelings at all? Is all anger sinful? There are many related questions with theological implications which we will consider in the discussion that follows.

WHAT IS ANGER? WHEN IS IT SINFUL?

Let's begin with the question, Is all anger sinful?

Obviously, not everything that can be identified under the heading of anger is violation of God's law, for Ephesians 4:26 instructs us to "be angry but do not sin" (*RSV*). That verse says to me that there is a difference between *strong feeling*, and the seething hostility which is consistently condemned in the Scripture. Our first task, it would appear, is to clarify that distinction.

Well, how about the emotion you experienced in the floral shop? You were no doubt angry when you walked toward the door. Was God displeased by what you were feeling?

I don't think so, and I felt no condemnation afterward. It's important to remember that anger is not only emotional—it is biochemical as well. The unprovoked assault by the store owner was perceived by me as enormously threatening. It didn't take an extended analysis to figure that out! In such a situation, the human body is equipped with an automatic defensive system, called the "flight or fight" mechanism, which prepares the entire organism for action. Adrenalin is pumped into the bloodstream which sets off a series of physiological responses within the body. Blood pressure is increased in accordance with an acceleration in heartbeat; the eyes are dilated for better peripheral vision; the hands get sweaty and the mouth gets dry; and the muscles are supplied with a sudden burst of energy. In a matter of seconds, the individual is transformed from a quiet condition to an "alarm reaction state." *Most importantly, this is an involuntary response which occurs whether or not we will it.*

Once the flight or fight hormones are released, it is impossible to ignore the intense feelings they precipitate. It would be like denying the existence of a toothache or any other tumultuous physical occurrence. And since God created this system as a means by which the body can protect itself against danger, I do not believe He condemns us for its proper functioning.

On the other hand, our *reaction* to the feeling of anger is more deliberate and responsive to voluntary control.

When we sullenly replay the agitating event over and over in our minds, grinding our teeth in hostility and seeking opportunities for revenge, or lash out in some overt act of violence, then it is logical to assume that we cross over the line into sinfulness. If this interpretation of the Scripture is accurate, then the exercise of the *will* stands in the gap between the two halves of the verse "be angry . . . do not sin."

Not all anger is caused by a threatening situation, is it? What about those responses that are brought on by extreme irritation or hostility?

All anger produces biochemical changes in the body, although the hormones released through irritating circumstances are somewhat different from the flight or fight system. I might also say that each individual has his own unique pattern of responses. Some people become overheated with the slightest provocation, and others are cool characters who seem to be born with an ability to stay "above it all." These differences are partially hereditary and partially conditioned by environmental circumstances during and after childhood.

But doesn't the Bible take an absolute position on the subject of anger? Where does it allow for the individual differences you described?

Didn't the apostle Paul write in Romans 12:18, "If it is possible, . . . live at peace with everyone"? In other words, we are all expected to exercise self-control and restraint, but some will be more successful than others by the nature of the individual temperaments. While we are at different levels of maturity and responsiblity, the Holy Spirit gently leads each of us in the direction He requires, until a moment of truth arrives when He demands our obedience.

How would you define the emotion of anger?

Anger is a complicated response which has become a sort of catchall phrase. Many of the behaviors which have been included under the heading of anger may have nothing to do with sinful behavior. Consider these examples:

Extreme fatigue produces a response which has the earmarks of anger. A mother who is exhausted from the day's activities can become very "angry" when her four-year-old spills his third glass of milk. This mother might give her very life for her child if required, and she would not harm a hair on his fuzzy little head. Nevertheless, her exhausted state of distress is given the same generalized label as the urge which caused Cain to kill Abel.

Extreme embarrassment typically produces a reaction which is categorized under the same worn-out heading. In fact, my reaction in the floral shop was motivated more by embarrassment than hostility for the toothy man who confronted me. I had no desire to hurt him either during or after the encounter. If the two of us had been alone, I think I could have coped with his assault more easily. Instead, there were six or eight onlookers who added the dimension of ego-loss to the episode.

Extreme frustration gives rise to an emotional response which we also call anger. I have seen this reaction from a high school basketball player, for example, who had an off night where everything went wrong. Perhaps he fumbled the ball away and double dribbled and missed all his shots at the basket. The more he tried, the worse he played and the more foolish he felt. Such frustration can trigger a volcanic emotional discharge at the coach or anyone in his way. Such are the irritations which cause golf clubs to be wrapped around trees and tennis rackets to be impaled on net-posts.

Rejection is another occurrence which often generates a kind of angry response. A girl who is jilted by the boy she loves, for example, may retaliate with a flurry of harsh words. Far from hating him, however, her response is motivated by the deep hurt associated with being thrown over—discarded—disrespected.

You see, anger has come to represent many strong, negative feelings in a human being. Accordingly, I doubt if all the Scriptures which address themselves to the subject of anger are referring equally to the entire range of emotions under that broad category.

Then how do the apparently innocent emotions you have described differ from sinful anger?

Your question raises a theological issue which may be difficult to communicate, yet it is of utmost importance to Christians everywhere. The Bible teaches the existence of a potentially disastrous flaw in the character of man which urges him toward sinful behavior, even though he may desire to serve God. Paul referred to this inner struggle in Romans 7:21-24: "So I find this law at work: When I want to do good, evil is right there with me. For in my inner being I delight in God's law; but I see another law at work in the members of my body, waging war against the law of my mind and making me a prisoner of the law of sin at work within my members. What a wretched man I am! Who will rescue me from this body of death?"

You see, Paul was speaking as a Christian, yet he admitted the existence of an internal war between good and evil. Anger, jealousy, envy, etc., are products of this inner nature. Paul was not unique in that regard, for the same predisposition has been inherited by the entire human race. David confessed, "In sin did my mother conceive me" (Ps. 51:5, *RSV*). It is, in effect, the "sin living in me" (Rom. 7:17) as opposed to sins which I commit.

Now, what does this have to do with the subject of anger? Simply this: our inbred sinful nature gives rise to a response that we might call "carnal anger" which must be distinguished from anger as a function of frustration or the endocrine system, or emotional and psychological needs. It is, instead, contrary to everything holy and righteous, *and cannot by any human striving be nullified.*

Virtually, every orthodox denomination acknowledges the biblical teaching I have described, for it is hardly escapable in the Scriptures. However, great disagreement occurs between Christians in regard to the *resolution* of the problem. The difference in teaching lies in whether or not it *can* be cleansed in this life and under what circumstances. It is my belief that the Holy Spirit, through an act of divine grace, cleanses and purifies the heart (see Acts 15:8,9) in order that the "body of sin might be rendered powerless" (Rom. 6:6).[1]

Do you believe that no further sin can occur after the evil nature has been removed?

No, the choice is still ours. Furthermore, it is obvious

that we remain subject to human frailty and foibles. We stumble into errors and fall short of God's best for our lives.

Paul asked a vital question in Romans 7:24, "Who will rescue me from this body of death?" (This body of death made reference to the Roman practice of tying a dead corpse to a person in such a way that he could not extricate himself from it—until the putrefying flesh eventually caused his own death.) Then Paul provided the glorious answer which is applicable to all mankind: "Thanks be to God—[I am rescued] through Jesus Christ our Lord!" (Rom. 7:24,25).

What are the characteristics of carnal anger? What aspect of it does God condemn in the Bible?

I see unacceptable anger as that which motivates us to hurt our fellowman—when we want to slash and cut and inflict pain on another person. Remember the experience of the apostle Peter when Jesus was being crucified. His emotions were obviously in a state of turmoil, seeing his beloved Master being subjected to an unthinkable horror. However, Jesus rebuked him when he severed the Roman soldier's ear with a sword. If there ever was a person with an excuse to lash out in anger, Peter seemed to be justified; nevertheless Jesus did not accept his behavior and He compassionately healed the wounded soldier.

There is a vitally important message for all of us in this recorded event. *Nothing* justifies an attitude of hatred or a desire to harm another person, and we are treading on dangerous ground when our thoughts and actions begin leading us in that direction. Not even the defense of Jesus Christ would justify that kind of aggression.

Are you saying that being "right" on an issue does not purify a wrong attitude or behavior?

Yes. In fact, having been in the church all my life, I've observed that Christians are often in greater danger when they are "right" in a conflict than when they are clearly wrong. In other words, a person is more likely to become bitter and deeply hostile when someone has cheated him or taken advantage of him than is the offender himself. E. Stanley Jones agreed, stating that a Christian is more likely to sin by his reactions than his actions. Perhaps this is one reason why Jesus told us to "turn the other cheek" and "go the second mile" (see Matt. 5:39,41), knowing that Satan can make devastating use of anger in an innocent victim.

If anger is unquestionably sinful when it leads us to hurt another person, then is the evil only involved in the aggressive act itself? What if we become greatly hostile but hold it inside where it is never revealed?

John told us that hatred for a brother is equivalent to murder (see 1 John 3:15). Thus, sinful anger can occur in the mind, even if it is never translated into overt behavior.

HOW DO YOU DEAL WITH ANGER?

Many psychologists seem to feel that all anger should be ventilated or verbalized. They say it is emotionally and physically harmful to repress or withhold any intense feeling. Can you harmonize

this scientific understanding with the scriptural commandment that "everyone should be quick to listen, slow to speak and slow to become angry" (Jas. 1:19).

Let me state the one thing of which I am absolutely certain: *Truth is unity.* In other words, when complete understanding is known about a given topic, then there will be no disagreement between science and the Bible. Therefore, when these two sources of knowledge appear to be in direct contradiction—as in the matter of anger—then there is either something wrong with our interpretation of Scripture or else the scientific premise is false. Under no circumstance, however, will the Bible be found to err. It was inspired by the Creator of the universe, and He does not make mistakes!

In regard to the psychological issues involved in the question, there is undoubtedly some validity to the current view that feelings of anger should not be encapsulated and internalized. When *any* powerful, negative emotion is forced from conscious thought while it is raging full strength, it has the potential of ripping and tearing us from within. The process by which we cram a strong feeling into the unconscious mind is called "repression," and it is psychologically hazardous. The pressure that it generates will usually appear elsewhere in the form of depression, anxiety, tension, or in an entire range of physical disorders.

On the other hand, it is my view that mental health workers have taken the above observation and carried it to ridiculous lengths. Professions of medicine, psychiatry, psychology, law, etc., go through fads and trends just like everything else involving human behavior. And for the past 10 years people working in the "helping sciences" have been obsessed by the need to express anger and resentment. It has almost become the all-time bogeyman of emotional illness, producing some strange recommendations for patients. Some therapists now urge their counselees to curse and slam their fists down on a table, until the expression of anger begins to feel "natural." This same philosophy was evident in a sixth-grade "alternative" classroom where I saw this statement written on the blackboard: "Hatred is stored-up anger. Therefore, getting mad is a loving thing." Another manifestation of this trend is seen in a popular book now available in the field of psychology which deals with "assertiveness training"— offering techniques for demanding and protecting one's rights. And finally, the women's liberation movement has spawned "consciousness raising groups" across America, which generate intense anger in response to the issues which women interpret as insulting to their gender.

In specific response to the question, we must harmonize the psychological finding that anger should be ventilated with the biblical commandment that we be "slow to become angry." Personally, I do not find these objectives to be in contradiction. God does not want us to repress our anger—sending it unresolved into the memory bank. Why else did the apostle Paul tell us to settle our irritations before sundown each day (see Eph. 4:26), effectively preventing an accumulation of seething hostility with the passage of time?

But how can intense negative feelings be resolved or ventilated without blasting away at the offender—an act which is specifically prohibited by the Scripture? Are there other ways of releasing pent-up emotions? Yes, including the following:

- by making the irritation a matter of prayer;
- by explaining our negative feelings to a mature and understanding third party who can advise and lead;
- by going to an offender and showing a spirit of love and forgiveness;
- by understanding that God often permits the most frustrating and agitating events to occur so as to teach us patience and help us grow;
- by realizing that *no* offense by another person could possibly equal our guilt before God, yet He has forgiven us; are we not obligated to show the same mercy to others?

These are just a few of the mechanisms and attitudes which act to neutralize a spirit of resentment.

The following question came to me in a letter from a person deeply concerned with the moral issues involved in the expression of anger:

I would like to have your opinion on a problem which is of much concern to me of late.

I have been seeing a psychologist for a few sessions because of an inferiority complex, low self-concept, timidity, insecurity and a nervous problem. I decided on my own to go to him, but I ran out of money and can't see him anymore.

Anyway, in the sessions he seemed to think that my problems stem from not expressing my irritations to those who irritate me because of fear of rejection by them. He feels I'm holding my irritations in when I should be letting them out. Also,

I'm single and do not have anyone for a scapegoat.

Now, he is a Christian psychologist, but his recommendation bothers me because it doesn't seem right. What do you think I should do?

Thank you for considering and replying to this letter.

While I don't have access to all the information available to the psychologist mentioned in this letter, it seems to me that he missed the point of this young woman's problem. Feelings of inferiority result primarily from the belief that you are unloved and disrespected by your friends and associates. This is agitated by suspicions of worthlessness, usually triggered by dissatisfaction with your body (I'm ugly!) or your mind (I'm dumb!) or through some area of social disgrace. A person with this gnawing sense of inadequacy has usually been a victim of poor relationships with people, and needs help in learning to rebuild those friendships.

From this perspective, then, what did the writer of this letter need less than an order to go home and bite everybody in sight? If she takes the advice of this well-meaning psychologist, she will soon be bearing a few teeth marks in return, which will hardly make her more confident!

Instead, I would have attempted to communicate this sort of message: "Life has been tough and you've had to struggle with it all by yourself. That is a difficult assignment for anyone to carry out. So from this point on, I'll help you handle the load. I don't have all the answers, but I have some of them, and we will face each new situation together. Most of all, I will show you some more successful ways of dealing with people and winning their support.

From this time forward, bring your most troubling frustrations to this room and we'll attack them systematically as a team."

I have a great deal of resentment and anger toward my father, for what he did to me and my mother when I was a child. I have struggled with these deep feelings for years; I don't want to hurt him, but I can't forget the pain he caused me and the rest of our family. How can I come to terms with this problem?

After laying the matter before God and asking for His healing touch, I would suggest that you examine the *perspective* in which you see your Dad. I attempted to explain this point in my book, *What Wives Wish Their Husbands Knew About Women*, and believe it will be helpful at this point:

A very close and respected friend of mine, whom I'll call Martha, has a father who has never revealed any depth of love for her. Though she is now grown and has two children of her own, she continues to hope that he will suddenly become what he has never been. This expectation causes Martha repeated disappointment and frustration. When her infant son failed to survive his first week of life, her insensitive father didn't even come to the funeral. He still shows little interest in Martha or her family—a fact which has caused deep wounds and scars through the years.

After receiving a letter from Martha in which she again mentioned her father's latest insult (he refused to come to her son's wedding), I sent her a few reactions and suggestions. She said she obtained so much help from what I had written that she shared it with three other women experiencing similar frustrations from people who have "failed" them. Finally, she returned a copy of my letter and asked me to include it in a future book of this nature. It appears below.

"Martha, I am more convinced every day that a great portion of our adult effort is invested in the quest for that which was *unreachable* in childhood. The more painful the early void, the more we are motivated to fill it later in life. Your dad never met the needs that a father should satisfy in his little girl, and I think you are still hoping he will miraculously become what he has never been. Therefore, he constantly disappoints you—hurts you—rejects you. I think you will be less vulnerable to pain when you accept the fact that he cannot, nor will he ever, provide the love and empathy and interest that he should. It is not easy to insulate yourself in this way. I'm still working to plug a few vacuums from my own tender years. *But it hurts less to expect nothing than to hope in vain.*

"I would guess that your dad's own childhood experiences account for his emotional peculiarities, and can perhaps be viewed as his own unique handicap. If he were blind, you would love him despite his lack of vision. In a sense, he is emotionally 'blind.' He is unable to see your needs. He is unaware of the hurt behind the unpleasant incidents and disagreements—the funeral of your baby, the disinterest in your life, and now Bob's wedding. His handicap makes it *impossible* for him to perceive your feelings and anticipation. If you can accept your father as a man with a permanent handicap—one which was probably caused when *he* was vulnerable—you will shield yourself from the ice pick of rejection.

"You didn't ask for this diatribe, and it may not hit your particular target at all. Nevertheless these are the thoughts which occurred to me as I read your letter.

"At least *we* are looking forward to the wedding. Martha. Best wishes to John and Bob and the entire Williams enterprise.

Sincerely,
Jim"

This letter was of help to Martha, but not because it improved her distressing circumstances. Her father is no more thoughtful and demonstrative today than he was in years past. It is Martha's *perspective* of him that has been changed. She now sees him as a victim of cruel forces in his own childhood which nicked and scarred his young psyche and caused him to insulate his emotions against the outside world. Since receiving this letter, Martha has learned that her father was subjected to some extremely traumatic circumstances during his childhood. (Among other things, his aunt told him unsympathetically that his father had died suddenly and then she reprimanded him severely for crying.) Martha's father is, as I suspected, a man with a handicap.[2]

How much self-control and Christian responsi-

bility can we expect of a child? For example, my five-year-old daughter has a rather passive personality, and she is constantly being hit, kicked and pinched by other children in the neighborhood. I have taught her not to fight back, showing her the words of Jesus in the Bible. Still, it hurts me to see her beaten—sometimes by children much smaller than she is. What do you suggest?

My views on this issue may be controversial, but I have developed them from observing the play of small children. Little people can be remarkably brutal and vicious to each other. They tend to think only of their own desires, resorting to power tactics to get what they want. In this competitive atmosphere, it is unrealistic to expect a young child to exhibit all of the characteristics of a mature Christian— turning the other cheek and walking the second mile. To require complete passivity from him is to strip his defenses in a world of fists and teeth and thrown fire trucks.

The relevant scriptural principles should be taught in the preschool years by a focus on *offensive* behavior, not defensive maneuvers. In other words, we should go to considerable lengths to teach our children not to hit and hurt others, and to be Christlike in their love. The second part of that formula (returning good for evil) requires greater maturity and a few more years.

I dealt with this same issue in my book, *Dare to Discipline*, wherein I discussed the fact that children respect power and strength. The following illustration is quoted in that context:

I recently consulted with a mother who was worried

about her small daughter's inability to defend herself. There was one child in their neighborhood who would crack three-year-old Ann in the face at the slightest provocation. This little bully, named Joan, was very small and feminine, but she never felt the sting of retaliation because Ann had been taught not to fight. I recommended that Ann's mother tell her to hit Joan back if she was hit first. Several days later the mother heard a loud altercation outside, followed by a brief scuffle. Then Joan began crying and went home. Ann walked casually into the house, with her hands in her pockets, and explained, "Joan socked me so I had to help her remember not to hit me again." Ann had efficiently returned an eye for an eye and a tooth for a tooth. She and Joan have played together much more peacefully since that time.

Generally speaking, a parent should emphasize the stupidity of fighting. But to force a child to stand passively while being clobbered is to leave him at the mercy of his cold-blooded peers.[3]

I have a very unhappy and miserable neighbor who can't get along with anybody. She has fought with everyone she knows at one time or another. I decided that I was going to make friends with her if it was humanly possible, so I went out of my way to be kind and compassionate. I thought I had made progress toward this goal until she knocked on the front door one day and attacked me verbally. She had misunderstood something I said to another neighbor, and she came to my house to "tell me

off." This woman said all the mean things she could think of, including some very insulting comments about my children, husband and our home.

I was agitated by her attempt to hurt me when I had tried to treat her kindly, and I reacted with irritation. We stood arguing with each other at the front door and then she left in a huff. I feel bad about the conflict now, but I don't know if I could handle it better today. What should have been my reaction?

Perhaps you realize that you missed the greatest opportunity you will probably ever have to accomplish your original objective of winning her friendship. It is difficult to convince someone of your love and respect during a period of shallow amicability. By contrast, your response to a vicious assault can instantly reveal the Christian values by which you live.

What if you had said, for example, "Mary, I don't know what you heard about me, but I think there's been a misunderstanding of what I said. Why don't you come in and we'll talk about it over a cup of coffee." Everything that you had attempted to accomplish through the previous months might have been achieved on that morning. I admit that it takes great courage and maturity to return kindness for hostility, but we are commanded by Jesus to do just that. He said in Matthew 5:43,44: "You have heard that it was said, 'Love your neighbor and hate your enemy.' But I tell you: Love your enemies and pray for those who persecute you."

I wish that I had been mature enough to have shown this spirit of Christ to the angry man in the floral shop. As I look back on the incident, I can understand much more clearly what caused its occurrence. There are three or four holidays during the year which are most difficult for a florist, and Easter is one of them. This poor man was probably exhausted from overwork and too little sleep. The hour that I arrived (5:00 P.M. Saturday) represented the point of greatest fatigue, but also maximum demands from the customers. I don't excuse his offensive behavior, but it had a definite *cause* which I should have comprehended.

I see him now, from the perspective of 10 years hence, as a hardworking fellow who was trying to earn a living and support his family. Jesus loves that man, and I must do the same. How I wish I had revealed the love of my heavenly Father in that moment of supreme *opportunity!*

What do you have to say to the many people who sincerely try to control their anger, but who get irritated and frustrated and still lose their temper time and time again? How can they bring this area under control? Or is it impossible?

I stated before that God dealt with me about my attitudes over a period of several years. He gave me gentle but firm leadership during that time, chastising me when I failed and speaking to me through the things I read, heard and experienced. But finally, there in the floral shop it all came to a head. As I said earlier, it seemed in that moment of conflict that the Lord asked, "Are you going to obey Me or not?"

It has been my observation that the Lord often leads us in a patient and progressively insistent manner. It begins with a mild sense of condemnation in the area where God wants us to grow and improve. Then as time goes by, a failure to respond is followed by a sense of guilt and awareness of divine disapproval. This stage leads to a period of intense awareness of God's requirements. We hear His message revealed (perhaps unwittingly) by the pastor on Sunday morning and in the books we read and even in secular programs on radio and television. It seems as though the whole world is organized to convey the same decree from the Lord. And finally, we come to a crisis point where God says, "You understand what I want. *Now do it!*"

Growth in the Christian life depends on obedience in those times of crisis. The believer who refuses to accept the new obligation despite unmistakable commandments from God is destined to deteriorate spiritually. From that moment forward, he begins to drift away from his Master. But for the Christian who accepts the challenge, regardless of how difficult it may be, his growth and enlightenment are assured.

John Henry Jowett said, "The will of God will never lead you where the grace of God cannot keep you." This means that the Lord won't demand something of you which He doesn't intend to help you implement.

I hope that this reply will be of encouragement to those who are facing struggles in this and related matters of self-control. The Christian experience is not an easy way of life—in no instance does the Bible teach that it is. Considerable discipline is required to love our enemies and maintain a consistent prayer life and exercise sexual control and give of our income to the work of the Lord—to name but a few of the many important areas of Christian responsibility. God doesn't expect instant maturity in each of these matters, but He does require consistent growth and improvement. The beautiful part is that we are not abandoned to struggle in solitude; the Holy Spirit "pities us as a father pities his child" (see Ps. 103:13), tenderly leading and guiding us in the paths of righteousness.

ASPECTS OF ANGER

Listed below are the aspects of anger which are most important to remember:

1. Strong negative feelings are accompanied by biochemical changes in the body, which are often set into motion by involuntary forces.

2. The word "anger" has come to represent a wide variety of emotions. Some of these feelings, such as responses to frustration, fatigue, embarrassment or rejection may not be sinful in the sight of God.

3. Carnal anger, by contrast, is motivated by an evil nature inherited by the entire human race. It is characterized by vindictiveness, hostility, resentment, and a desire to hurt or damage another person. This reaction, whether expressed or hidden, is resoundingly condemned in the Bible.

4. A Christian can be in greater spiritual danger when he has been a victim than when he was the aggressor. *Nothing* justifies an attitude of bitterness.

5. Strong negative feelings should not be repressed or pushed into the unconscious mind, but should be released in a manner that is not spiritually destructive or harmful to another person.

6. Distressing negative feelings can often be pacified and eliminated by recognizing the human vulnerability and frailty of the person who offends us. This is the "Christian perspective," and can be learned with the help of the Holy Spirit.

7. Christians differ in the degree to which they manifest the characteristics of a mature relationship with God. Each willing person is led by the Holy Spirit toward greater Christlikeness.

8. There is no greater opportunity to influence our fellowman for Christ than to respond with love when we have been unmistakably wronged and assaulted. On those occasions, the difference between Christian love and the values of the world are most brilliantly evident.

"Your attitude should be the same as that of Christ Jesus" (Phil. 2:5).

LEARNING-DISCUSSION IDEAS

What Is Anger? When Is It Sinful?

1. After relating the incident in the floral shop, Dr. Dobson raises the question: Is all anger sinful? What is your opinion? Why?

2. List three times you remember being angry. Think through how you expressed your anger. What did you do? What did you say? How would you label your responses in each incident: controlled? uncontrolled?

What ideas for handling anger can you find in Ephesians 4:26,27; Proverbs 29:11?

3. Dr. Dobson states: "It's important to remember

that anger is not only emotional—it is biochemical as well."
Does this mean that angry feelings are sometimes beyond
our control? What about angry actions? What does Psalm
37:8 suggest to you about angry actions?

4. Why is counting to 10 (or 100!) a good idea when
angry feelings are strong? What biochemical advantage
does it give you? How does Proverbs 29:11 apply?

5. In defining the emotion of anger, Dr. Dobson gives
four causes of angry feelings. List the causes. Which of the
causes have you experienced? In Galatians 5:22-26 what
ideas do you find that can help you deal with anger that
results from extreme fatigue, embarrassment, frustration
and rejection?

6. Read Romans 7:21 and draw a sketch or diagram
that illustrates what this Scripture verse suggests to you
regarding your experiences with controlling anger.

7. Using the following Scripture references make a list
of five or more expressions of anger that God's Word
condemns: Colossians 3:8; Ephesians 4:31; Proverbs
29:22.

8. What does James 1:19,20 say about God's view of
anger?

How Do You Deal with Anger?

1. Write a brief description of something that recently
made you angry. How could you have handled the situation using the principle advocated by many psychologists:
angry feelings should be released and anger ventilated?
How could you have handled the same situation using the
biblical principle: be "slow to become angry"? Talk with a

partner or the group. Can both principles be used in the same situation? How?

2. According to Dr. Dobson, are the following statements true or false?

● Even if your position is right, your attitude can be wrong.

● When someone is angry with you, the hostile, bitter reaction you may experience might be justified.

● Christians should always repress anger and avoid expressing strong feelings.

● Recognizing the problems of the other person helps you control your negative, angry feelings.

Discuss each statement and your answer with a partner or group.

3. The Bible has much to say about angry feelings and hostile actions. Study the following Scripture references. Underline ideas that give you personal help in handling your own feelings of anger: Psalm 4:4; Proverbs 14:29; 15:1,18; 19:11 and 29:11; Ecclesiastes 7:7-9; Matthew 5:22; Romans 12:19,21; 14:13; Ephesians 4:26,31,32; Colossians 3:8,10.

4. Do you have feelings of anger and hostility you want to change? Try this. Read Galatians 5:22,23; Matthew 7:1 and Romans 14:13. Then pray and thank God for His promise of forgiveness. Ask Him to replace your critical feelings with the characteristics of His Spirit.

5. Choose one or two of the following suggestions for ways you can move to change your angry and hostile feelings: (a) list personal reasons why you want to give up your angry feelings about a certain situation; (b) decide on the most important reason and underline it; (c) plan two

specific ways you are going to act to change your behavior;
(d) memorize Ephesians 4:30-32 or write out the verses
and hang the paper where you will see it often.

6. Dr. Dobson says a person is less apt to feel anger if
he is able to accept the other person as he is. Discuss this
view with your partner or group. Do you agree or disagree
with Dobson's statement? Why? It sounds simple to "accept the other person as he is." Is this easy to do? Or
difficult? Why? How does John 15:12 encourage the
Christian to be acceptant of others?

7. According to Dr. Dobson, controlling anger is a
valuable opportunity for communicating love and respect.
Can you think of a time when anger between you and a
member of your family gave you an opportunity to communicate love and respect? How did you use that opportunity? Visualize yourself angry with the same person
again. What do you see yourself doing? How can a person
communicate love and respect in the midst of anger?

Dobson encourages the Christian to remember: "God
doesn't expect instant maturity in these matters, but He
does require consistent growth and improvement." Write
out your personal goals for growth and improvement on
handling anger in your family relationships.

Notes

1. Other theological positions on this issue include: the evil nature can only be
purified after death in purgatory; the inherited depravity is purged in the hour
and article of death; man's sinful nature is brought under control as he trusts
Christ and is sanctified by the work of the Holy Spirit; a cleansing is accomplished
by the Holy Spirit through the years in a process of Christian growth.

2. James Dobson, *What Wives Wish Their Husbands Knew About Women*
(Wheaton, IL: Tyndale House Publishers, 1975), pp. 181-183.

3. James Dobson, *Dare to Discipline* (Wheaton, IL: Tyndale House Publishers, 1970), pp. 179, 180.

For Further Reading

Ahlem, Lloyd H. *How to Cope*. Ventura, CA: Regal Books, 1978. Tells how to cope with fear, conflict, stress, guilt, crisis and change.

Augsburger, David. *Caring Enough to Confront, rev. ed.* Ventura, CA: Regal Books, 1980. Discusses conflict, anger, blame, guilt and describes a Christian life-style that cares enough to confront others when differences arise.

Osborne, Cecil. *The Art of Understanding Yourself*. Grand Rapids: Zondervan Publishing House, 1968. A blend of Christian principles and psychology to help you understand why you feel the way you do and how to live a full and peaceful life.

Wise, Robert L. *Your Churning Place*. Ventura, CA: Regal Books, 1977. Tells how to cope with and defeat guilt, self-centeredness, escapism, change, jealousy and anxiety.

Wright, H. Norman. *The Christian Use of Emotional Power*. Old Tappan, NJ: Fleming H. Revell, 1974. Chapter 6, "Make the Most of Your Anger," examines the causes, types and effects of anger upon daily interpersonal relationships. Gives scriptural and psychological guidance on handling anger.

PART IV

Interpretation of Impressions

- Can we trust our impressions in interpreting the will of God?
- Under what circumstances does God speak directly to the heart of man?
- Does Satan also speak directly on occasion? If so, how can the two voices be distinguished?
- What role does fatigue and illness play in the interpretation of impressions?
- How can major decisions be made without leaning too heavily on ephemeral emotions?

CAN YOU KNOW GOD'S WILL?

How do you determine God's specific will for your life? This may be *the* most important question which will confront you as a Christian, for therein lies the key to obedience. You can hardly obey God if you are hazy about His leadership in your daily experience. But how can divine purposes be known absolutely? By what method can you be certain of His specific approval and disapproval? How do you know that your attitudes and home and way of life are pleasing to Him?

From my discussions with Christians, it appears that God's will is most often determined by inner feelings and impressions. "I just felt this is what God wanted me to do," is a typical explanation. Thus, a fleeting emotion or a subtle impression may lead a person to accept or reject a job, move to a different city, return to college or even plunge into marriage. From the flimsiest evidence, we conclude: "God told me" or "God sent me" or "God required me." But how valid are such impressions? Does God always speak through this voice from within? Is it possible to "hear" a false message from the Lord?

In this chapter we will discuss the psychological and spiritual forces that affect our understanding of God's specific leading and guidance for our lives.

WHY YOU CAN'T TRUST
INNER FEELINGS AND IMPRESSIONS

Can you give some examples of how inner feel-

ings and impressions can mislead and confuse someone who is genuinely trying to serve the Lord?

The subject of impressions always reminds me of the exciting day I completed my formal education at the University of Southern California and was awarded a doctoral degree. My professors shook my hand and offered their congratulations, and I walked from the campus with the prize I had sought so diligently. On the way home in the car that day, I expressed my appreciation to God for His obvious blessing on my life, and I asked Him to use me in any way He chose. The presence of the Lord seemed very near as I communed with Him in that little red Volkswagen.

Then, as I turned a corner (I remember the precise spot), I was seized by a strong impression which conveyed this unmistakable message: "You are going to lose someone very close to you within the next 12 months. A member of your immediate family will die, but when it happens, don't be dismayed. Just continue trusting and depending on Me."

Since I had not been thinking about death or anything that would have explained the sudden appearance of this premonition, I was alarmed by the threatening thought. My heart thumped a little harder as I contemplated who might die and in what manner the end would come. Nevertheless, I told no one about the experience when I reached my home that night.

One month passed without tragedy or human loss. Two and three months sped by, and still the hand of death failed to visit my family. Finally, the anniversary of my morbid impression came and went without consequence. It has now been more than a decade since that frightening day in the Volkswagen, and there have been no catastrophic events in either my family or among my wife's closest relatives. The impression has proved invalid.

Through my subsequent counseling experience and professional responsibilities, I have learned that my phony impression was not unique. Similar experiences are common, particularly among those who have not adjusted well to the challenge of living.

For example, a 30-year-old wife and mother came to me for treatment of persistent anxiety and depression. In relating her history she described an episode that occurred in a church service when she was 16 years old. Toward the end of the sermon, she "heard" this alarming message from God: "Jeanie, I want you to die so that others will come to Me."

Jeanie was absolutely terrified. She felt as though she stood on the gallows with the hangman's noose dangling above her head. In her panic, she jumped from her seat and fled through the doors of the building, sobbing as she ran. Jeanie felt she would commit a sin if she revealed her impression to anyone, so she kept it to herself. For nearly 20 years she had awaited the execution of this divine sentence, still wondering when the final moment would arrive. Nevertheless, she appeared to be in excellent health many years later.

Not only do death messages sometimes prove to be unreliable, but other apparent statements of God's will can be equally misunderstood. In the chapter on romantic love I mentioned a college student who was awakened from a dream in the middle of the night with a strong impression that he should marry a certain young lady. They had only dated once or twice and hardly knew each other—yet, "God" assured him "this is the one!" The next morning, he called the coed and told her of his midnight encounter. The girl felt no such impulse, but didn't want to oppose so definite a message from the Lord. The young man and woman were married shortly thereafter, and have suffered through the agony of an unsuccessful and stormy marriage.

From the examples I have cited and dozens more, I have come to regard the interpretation of impressions as risky business, at best.

Are you saying that God does not speak directly to the heart—that all impressions are false and unreliable?

Certainly not. It is the expressed purpose of the Holy Spirit to deal with human beings in a most personal and intimate way, convicting and directing and influencing. However, some people seem to find it very difficult to distinguish the voice of God from other sounds within.

Do some of those "other sounds" represent the influence of Satan?

We are told in 2 Corinthians 11:14 that the devil comes to us as "an angel of light," which means he counterfeits the work of the Holy Spirit. This is why he is described in profoundly evil terms in the Bible, leaving little room for doubt as to his motives or nature. His character is presented as wicked, malignant, subtle, deceitful, fierce and cruel. He is depicted as a wolf, roaring lion and a serpent. Among the titles ascribed to Satan are these: "Murderer,"

"Dragon," "Old Serpent," "Wicked One," "Liar,"
"Prince of the Devils," and more than 20 other names
which describe a malicious and incomparably evil nature.

These scriptural descriptions of Satan are written for a
purpose: we should recognize that the "Father of Lies" has
earned his reputation at the expense of those he has
damned! And there is no doubt in my mind that he often
uses destructive impressions to implement his evil
purposes.

**You said your premonition of impending death
occurred while you were praying. Is it really possible for Satan to speak in the midst of an earnest
prayer?**

Was not Jesus tempted by Satan while He was on a
40-day prayer and fasting journey in the wilderness?

Yes, the devil can speak at any time. Let me go a step
further: harmful impressions can bear other earmarks of
divine revelation. They can occur and recur for months at a
time. They can be as intense as any other emotion in life.
They can be verified by Christian friends and can even
seemingly be validated by striking passages of Scripture.

**Would you give an example of how Satan uses a
false notion to cause spiritual damage?**

A man with six children became a Christian and, in his
spiritual immaturity, felt he was "called' to the ministry.
He quit his job the next week, even though he had no
financial reserves and had hardly been able to provide
necessities for his wife and children. By scraping together
every available penny, the family moved across the state to

allow the father to attend a Christian college. From the beginning, one disaster followed another. Sick children, work layoffs, academic troubles, physical exhaustion and marital discord accumulated day by day until life became utterly intolerable. Finally, the father quit school and admitted that he had made an enormous mistake. More importantly, his spiritual enthusiasm had been extinguished in the process—an object lesson that was carefully observed by his six children. (I should emphasize that the "call" of this man to the ministry could have been genuine, and the troubles he faced do not necessarily disprove its validity. But from a strictly human point of view, it appears that he responded impulsively and unwisely to his inner feelings and impressions.)

The Christian who accepts his own impressions at face value—uncritically—is extremely vulnerable to satanic mischief. He is obligated to implement every obsession, regardless of how ridiculous or demanding it seems. He is compelled by a little voice from within which warns, "Do this or else," stripping him of judgment and reason.

Are some impressions and feelings of our own making?

In a way they all are. By that I mean that all of our impulses and thoughts are vulnerable to our physical condition and psychological situation at any given moment. Haven't you noticed that your impressions are affected by the amount of sleep you had last night, and the state of your health, and your level of confidence at that time, and dozens of other forces which impinge upon your decision-making processes? We are trapped in these "earthen ves-

sels," and our perception is necessarily influenced by our
humanness.

**I have sometimes wondered if my impressions
don't obediently tell me what I most want to hear.
For example, I felt greatly led to take a new job that
offered a higher salary and shorter working hours.**

That reminds me of the minister who received a call to
a much larger and stronger church than he ever expected
to lead. He replied, "I'll pray about it while my wife packs."

It is very difficult to separate the "want to" from our
interpretation of God's will. The human mind will often
obediently convince itself of anything in order to have its
own way. Perhaps the most striking example of this self-
delusion occurred with a young couple who decided to
engage in sexual intercourse before marriage. Since the
young man and woman were both reared in the church,
they had to find a way to lessen the guilt from this forbidden act. So, they actually got down on their knees and
prayed about what they were going to do, and received
"assurance" that it was all right to continue!

**I notice that spiritual discouragement and de-
feat are much more common when I am tired than
when I am rested. Is this characteristic of others?**

When a person is exhausted he is attacked by ideas he
thought he conquered long ago. The great former football
coach for the Green Bay Packers, Vince Lombardi, once
told his team why he pushed them so hard toward proper
physical conditioning. He said, "Fatigue makes cowards of
us all." He was absolutely right. As the reserves of human

energy are depleted, one's ability to reject distressing thoughts and wild impressions is greatly reduced.

You mentioned the man who dreamed that he should marry a certain woman. Does God ever speak to us through dreams today?

I don't know. He certainly used this method of communicating in Old Testament times; however, it appears to me that the use of dreams has been less common since the advent of the Holy Spirit, because the Spirit was sent to be our source of enlightenment (see John 16).

Even in prior times, Jeremiah called dreams "chaff" when compared to the Word of God. Personally, I would not accept a dream as being authentic, regardless of how vivid it seemed, until the same content was verified in other ways.

What do you mean by having the "content verified in other ways"?

I mean that the "direction" given to me in a dream should be supported by other pieces of information that I would receive. For example, suppose I dream that I am called to Africa as a medical missionary. Before I start packing, I should consider some other factors: Am I qualified by training, experience, interests? Have there been any direct invitations or opportunities presented?

John Wesley wrote in the nineteenth century, "Do not hastily ascribe things to God. Do not easily suppose dreams, voices, impressions, visions or revelations to be from God. They may be from Him. They may be nature. They may be from the Devil. Therefore, believe not every spirit, but 'try the spirits whether they be from God.' "

From a psychological point of view, dreams appear to have two basic purposes: they reflect wish fulfillment, giving expression to the things we long for; and they ventilate anxiety and the stresses we experience during waking hours. From a strictly physiological point of view, dreams also serve to keep us asleep when we are drifting toward consciousness. Dreams are being studied at length in experimental laboratories today, although their nature is still rather poorly understood.

If what we feel is so unreliable and dangerous, then how can we ever know the will of God? How can we tell the difference between the leadings of the Holy Spirit and subtle, evil influences of Satan, himself?

Let's look to the Scripture for a word of encouragement:

Concerning Christ's power to help in time of temptation: "Because he himself suffered when he was tempted, he is able to help those who are being tempted" (Heb. 2:18).

Concerning the power of God to convey His will to us: "And this is my prayer. That the God of our Lord Jesus Christ, the all-glorious Father, will give you spiritual wisdom and the insight to know more of him: that you may receive that inner illumination of the spirit which will make you realize how great is the hope to which he is calling you—the magnificence and splendor of the inheritance promised to Christians—and how tremendous is the power available to us who believe in God" (Eph. 1:16-19, *Phillips*).

Concerning the power of God over Satan: "You, my children, who belong to God have already defeated them, because the one who lives in you is stronger than the anti-Christ in the world" (1 John 4:4, *Phillips*).

Concerning the divine promise to lead and guide us: "I will instruct thee and teach thee in the way which thou shalt go: I will guide thee with mine eye" (Ps. 32:8, *KJV*).

In paraphrased form, these four Scriptures offer these promises:

1. Jesus was tempted by Satan when He was on earth, so He is fully equipped to deal with him now on our behalf.

2. "Inner illumination" and "spiritual wisdom" are made available to us by the God who controls the entire universe.

3. Satan's influence is checkmated by the omniscient power of God living within us.

4. Like a father leading his trusting child, our Lord will guide our steps and teach us His wisdom.

These four Scriptures are supported by dozens more which promise God's guidance, care and leadership in our lives.

Then how do you account for the experiences of those Christians who grope with uncertainty in the darkness and eventually stumble and fall? How do you explain incidents whereby Satan traps them into believing and acting on his lies?

The Scripture, again, provides its own answer to that

troubling question. We are told in 1 John 4:1: "Dear friends, do not believe every spirit, but test the spirits to see whether they are from God." A similar commandment is given in 1 Thessalonians 5:21: "Test everything. Hold on to the good." In other words, it is our responsibility to test and prove all things—including the validity of our impressions. To do otherwise is to give Satan an opportunity to defeat us, despite the greater power of the Holy Spirit who lives within. We would not have been told to test the spirits if there were no danger in them.

HOW TO TEST INNER FEELINGS AND IMPRESSIONS

By what means can I test my own feelings and impressions? What are the steps necessary to prove the will of God?

The best answer I've read for those questions was written in 1892 by Martin Wells Knapp. In his timeless little booklet entitled *Impressions,* he described those impulses and leadings that come from above (from God) versus those that originate from below (from Satan). Just as the Holy Spirit may tell us by impressions what His will is concerning us, so also can our spiritual enemies tell us by impressions what their will is. And unfortunately, there is often a striking resemblance between the two kinds of messages. According to Knapp, one of the objectives of Satan is to get the Christian to lean totally on his impressions, accepting them uncritically as the absolute voice of God. When this occurs, "the devil has got all he wants."

When seeking God's will Knapp recommends that each impression be evaluated very carefully to see if it reflects four distinguishing features:

Scriptural. Is the impression in harmony with the Bible? Guidance from the Lord is *always* in accordance with the Holy Scripture, and this gives us an infallible point of reference and comparison. If this test had been applied by the young couple that was contemplating sexual permissiveness, mentioned earlier, they would have known that the "approval" they obtained was not from the Lord. Furthermore, the numerous religious movements which obviously add to Scripture or contradict its primary concepts would not have been born if the Bible had been accepted as the ultimate and complete Word of God.

The most important aspect of this first test is that *the entire Bible be used* instead of the selection of "proof texts" or "chance texts." A reader can find support for almost any viewpoint if he lifts individual verses or partial phrases out of context. We are commanded to study the Scriptures, not toy with them or manipulate them for our own purposes.

Right. Knapp's second test of impressions involves the matter of rightness. "Impressions which are from God are always right," says Knapp. "They may be contrary to our feelings, our prejudices and our natural inclinations, but they are always right. They will stand all tests."[1]

I am acquainted with a family that was destroyed by an impression that could not have passed the test: *Is it right?* Although there were four little children in the home, the mother felt she was "called" to leave them and enter full-time evangelistic work. On very short notice she abandoned the children who needed her so badly and left them in the care of their father who worked six and seven days a week.

The consequence was devastating. The youngest in the family lay awake at night, crying for his mommy. The older children had to assume adult responsibilities which they were ill-prepared to carry. There was no one at home to train and love and guide the development of the lonely little family. I simply cannot believe the mother's impression was from God because it was neither scriptural nor "right" to leave the children. I suspect that she had other motives for fleeing her home, and Satan provided her with a seemingly noble explanation to cover her tracks.

As Knapp said, "Millions of impressions, if compelled to answer the simple question, 'Are you right?' will blush and hesitate and squirm, and finally in confusion, retire."

Providential. In explaining the importance of providential circumstances, Knapp quoted Hannah Whitall Smith, writing in *The Christian's Secret of a Happy Life*: "If a leading is from the Holy Spirit, 'the way will always open for it.' The Lord assures us of this when he says: 'When he putteth forth his own sheep, he goeth before them, and the sheep follow him: for they know his voice' (John 10:4). Notice here the expression 'goeth before' and 'follow.' He goes before to open the way, and we are to follow in the way thus opened. It is never a sign of divine leading when a Christian insists on opening his own way, and riding roughshod over all opposing things. If the Lord goes before us he will open all doors before us, and we shall not need ourselves to hammer them down."

Reasonable. The apostle Paul referred to the Christian

life as a "reasonable service." Accordingly, the will of God can be expected to be in harmony with *spiritually enlightened judgment.* We will not be asked to do absurd and ridiculous things which are devoid of judgment and common sense. Knapp said, "God has given us reasoning powers for a purpose, and he respects them, appeals to them, and all of his leadings are in unison with them."

Perhaps, the most common violation of this principle is seen in the pressure some people feel to force every chance conversation into a heaven-or-hell confrontation. Such individuals believe they *must* witness in every elevator, preach to any available group of four or more, and turn every routine encounter into an altar service. Of course, each Christian should "be prepared to give an answer" when the opportunity is provided, but the gospel should be shared in a natural and tactful manner.

Another frequent disregard for the test of reason is seen with *impulsive* behavior. It was Knapp's view, and I heartily agree, that God deals with us as rational beings and He rarely requires us to act on sudden suggestions or impressions. G.D. Watson stated it similarly, "The devil wants you to be in a hurry and rush and go pell mell and not wait for anything; whereas Jesus is always quiet and He is always calm and always takes His time." Likewise, the psalmist David instructed us to "wait on the Lord."

Of Knapp's four criteria, "providential circumstances" seems hardest to apply. Can you give an example?

Personally, I have come to depend heavily on providential circumstances to speak to me of God's will. My impressions serve as little more than "hunches" which cause me to pay closer attention to more concrete evidence around me. For example, in 1970 my wife and I considered the wisdom of selling our house and buying one better suited to the needs of our growing family. However, there are many factors to consider in such a move. The life-style, values and even the safety of a family are influenced by the neighborhood in which they reside. I felt it would be foolish to sell our home and buy a new one without seeking the specific guidance of the Lord.

After making the possibility a matter of prayer, I felt I should offer our house for sale without listing it with a realtor. If it sold I would know that God had revealed His leading through this providential circumstance. For two weeks a *For Sale* sign stood unnoticed in the front yard. It didn't attract a single call or knock on the door, and my prayer was answered in the negative.

I took down the sign and waited 12 months before asking the same question of the Lord. This time, the house sold for my asking price without a nickle being spent on advertising or real estate fees. There was no doubt in my mind that the Lord had another home in mind for us.

How do you know that the sale of the house was not explained by economic circumstances or simply by the fact that an interested buyer came along? Can you say, definitely, that God determined the outcome?

Matters of faith can never be proved; they always have to be "the substance of things hoped for, the evidence of things not seen" (Heb. 11:1 *KJV*). It would be impossible to make a skeptic acknowledge that God influenced the sale of my house, just as the same unbeliever would doubt my conversion experience wherein I became a Christian. You see, it was not the unadvertised sale of my house that convinced me that God was involved in the issue—it was that I met with Him on my knees in prayer and asked for His specific guidance and direction. I have reason to believe that He cares about me and my family and hears me when I ask for His leadership. Therefore, my interpretation of the event is based not on facts but on faith. Spiritual experiences must *always* rest on that foundation.

Incidentally, there is a sequel to the "house" story. As I was driving to the hospital a month later, I thanked God for letting me know His purposes and will for my family. As I prayed, however, it occurred to me that the Lord had sold my house, making Him entitled to the fee that I would have paid a real estate agent. That is another way of saying that God was entitled to my tithe (a portion of the profit) since I sold the house for more than I paid for it. Knowing the tyranny of impressions, I immediately uttered this prayer: "Lord, if this is you talking to me, then give me the same message from another source. I will mention it to no one, but I will be listening for your instructions in every area of my life."

The following Sunday, I told an adult class at my church how the Lord had answered my prayer through the sale of the house. I said nothing about the impression that I should give $1,600 to the church. After class, however, I received the following note from one of the young men who had heard me: "Don't you think God is entitled to a 'real estate fee' for selling your house?" He meant it as a joke, but his humor encouraged me to give the $1,600 the following week.

I have found security in this method of exploring God's will. In essence, my attitude to the Lord is simply this: "I will do *anything* you require of me. *Anything*! I only ask that you convey your will in a definite manner that requires a minimum of reliance on my unpredictable feelings." He has usually satisfied the request.

Returning to the views of Knapp regarding the providential circumstances, he says, "God never impresses a Noah to build an ark, or a Solomon to build a temple, but that means, material and men await their approaching faith. He never impresses a Philip to go preach to an individual but that He prepares the person for Philip's preaching. He never says to an imprisoned Peter, 'arise up quickly,' but that Peter will find chains providentially burst."

In essence, then, the test of providential circumstances allows us to "read" the will of God by interpreting the opportunities and events which surround us.

Will there be times when the application of Knapp's four tests still leaves a Christian in a state of doubt about the leadings of the Lord? Or does a committed Christian always know precisely what God wants of him?

Your question is one which is rarely confronted in books dealing with the will of God, but I feel we must meet it head-on. I believe there are times in the lives of most believers when confusion and perplexity are rampant. What could Job have felt, for example, when his world began to crack and splinter? His family members were killed in a tragic manner, his livestock was wiped out, and he was besieged by boils from the top of his head to the bottom of his feet. But most troubling of all was his inability to make spiritual sense of the circumstances. He knew he hadn't sinned, despite the accusations of his "friends," yet God must have seemed a million miles away. He said at one point, "Oh, that I knew where to find God—that I could go to his throne and talk with him there" (Job 23:3, *TLB*). "But I search in vain. I seek him here, I seek him there, and cannot find him. I seek him in his workshop in the North, but cannot find him there; nor can I find him in the South; there, too, he hides himself" (Job 23:8,9, *TLB*).

Was this experience unique to Job? I don't think so. In my counseling responsibilities with Christian families, I've learned that sincere, dedicated believers go through tunnels and storms, too. We inflict a tremendous disservice on young Christians by making them think only sinners experience confusion and depressing times in their lives. Apparently, God permits these difficult moments for our own edification. James wrote, "Consider it pure joy, my brothers, whenever you face trials of many kinds, because you know that the testing of your faith develops perseverence" (Jas. 1:2,3).

We must remember that God is not a subservient genie who comes out of a bottle to sweep away each trial and hurdle that blocks our path. He has not promised to lay out an eight-year master plan that delineates every alternative in the roadway. Rather, He offers us His will for *today* only. Our tomorrows must be met one day at a time, negotiated with a generous portion of faith.

Are you saying there will be times in a Christian's life when God's will and actions may not make sense to him?

Yes, and I regret the shallow teaching today which denies this fact. We are told in the book of Isaiah, "For my thoughts are not your thoughts, neither are your ways my ways, declares the Lord" (Isa. 55:8). Furthermore, the apostle Paul verified that "now we see but a poor reflection." In practical terms, this means that there will be times when God's behavior will be incomprehensible and confusing to us. *More explicitly, there will be occasions when God will seem to contradict Himself.*

One of the brightest young men ever to graduate from my collegiate alma mater was deeply devoted to the Lord. He felt called to become a medical missionary and he directed every energy toward that objective. After graduating cum laude from college, he enrolled in medical school and finished his first year at the very top of his class, academically. Then during the spring of that year he began to experience a curious and persistent fatigue. He was examined by a physician who made the diagnosis of leukemia. The promising student was dead a few months later.

How can a tragedy like that be explained? The Lord seemed to call him to the mission field where his healing talents were desperately needed. He was accepted into medical school despite fierce competition. Every step seemed to be ordered by God. Then, suddenly, he was taken. What did the Lord have in mind from the beginning? Why did He seem to give him a definite call and then frustrate its culmination? I have no idea. I simply offer this illustration as one of thousands where God's actions are difficult for us to explain in simplistic terms. And in these moments we have to say with Job, "Though he slay me, yet will I trust in him."

Are we to conclude, then, that there are occasions when we will pray for the will of God to be known and yet we may "hear" no immediate reply?

I think so, but I'm also convinced that God is as close to us and as involved in our situation during those times when we feel nothing as He is when we are spiritually exhilarated. We are not left to flounder. Rather our faith is strengthened by these testing periods. The only comforting attitude to hold during these stressful times is beautifully summarized in 2 Corinthians 4:8-10: "We are pressed on every side by troubles, but not crushed and broken. We are perplexed because we don't know why things happen as they do, but we don't give up and quit. We are hunted down, but God never abandons us. We get knocked down, but we get up again and keep going. These bodies of ours are constantly facing death just as Jesus did; so it is clear to all that it is only the living Christ within [who keeps us safe]" (*TLB*).

Are there other biblical examples of instances when the will of God was strange or contradictory to His faithful followers?

The Scripture is replete with such illustrations. Think of the experiences of the faithful man of God, Abraham. He had been promised a miracle-child, but Sarah remained barren throughout her reproductive years. She ex-

perienced menopause without the realization of the blessing, and Abraham began to grow old and wrinkled. He was
nearly 100 and Sarah was over 90, but still no child came.
Did the Lord visit Abraham frequently during those long
years to reassure him that He hadn't forgotten His promise? We have no record of such communication. To a man
of lesser faith it would have been clear that God had
foolishly contradicted Himself. But Abraham patiently
waited for the fulfillment of prophecy.

The greatest contradiction was yet to come, however.
After the promised child was finally born—the one in
whom all the prophecies of blessing were to be fulfilled—
then God curiously required Abraham to sacrifice his precious son as a burnt offering. What a fantastic contradiction! How could Abraham become the father of many
nations and be blessed by the eventual birth of the Messiah
if his only legitimate child was to die? There is no way that
Abraham could have understood this event as it unfolded,
and he must have been thoroughly confused during those
perplexing days. God made no sense at all. Nevertheless,
Abraham remained obedient and faithful in every detail,
even to the moment the angel of God spared Isaac's life.

Here is the beautiful part of the familiar story, and the
portion which is most relevant to our discussion about the
will of God. To Abraham, the future depended upon Isaac.
All the promises seemed to rest on this miracle-child. But
God was showing Abraham that the future did not rest with
Isaac—it belonged to *God*. That fact is as true for us today
as it was for the father of the Jewish nation! The future does
not depend on our jobs or our health or our stocks and
bonds; it rests in the hands of the Almighty. Even when

divine providence seems senseless and contradictory, even when the death of a loved one is without explanation, even when financial reverses threaten our security, even when pain and hardship pose unanswerable questions—even then, the future belongs to God. He has not forgotten us and His plan has not been thwarted. It is our responsibility in those uncertain moments to remain faithful and obedient, awaiting His revelation and reassurance.

Let's return to the words of Job in his moment of supreme trial. Despite the miserable and perplexing circumstances which engulfed him, his faith reached through the oppressive darkness and grasped the promises of God: "But he knoweth the way that I take [he knows where I am]; when he hath tried me, I shall come forth as gold" (Job 23:10, *KJV*).

HOW TO KNOW GOD'S WILL

How can we know, definitely, the purposes and leadings of the Lord for our lives? Here are key points to remember:

● Many Christians depend exclusively on their impressions to determine the will of God.

● However, not all impressions are valid. Some are from God; some are from Satan; some are probably of our own making.

● Since it is difficult to determine the origin of an impression, we can easily make a mistake while assuming that a feeling is sent from God.

● Our Lord has promised to enlighten us and "guide

us with his eye." On the other hand, He wants us to "test" our impressions and leadings.

• Therefore, every impression should be tested by four criteria before being accepted as valid:

1. Is it scriptural? This test involves more than taking a random proof text. It means studying what the whole Bible teaches. Use a concordance, search the Scriptures as did the Bereans (see Acts 17:11). Evaluate tentative leanings against the immutable Word of God.

2. Is it right? Every expression of God's will can be expected to conform to God's universal principles of morality and decency. If an impression would result in the depreciation of human worth or the integrity of the family or related traditional Christian values, it must be viewed with suspicion.

3. Is it providential? The third test requires every impression to be considered in the light of providential circumstances, such as: are the necessary doors opening or closing? Do circumstances permit the implementation of what I feel to be God's will? Is the Lord speaking to me through events?

4. Is it reasonable? The final criterion against which the will of God is measured relates to the appropriateness of the act. Does it make sense? Is it consistent with the character of God to require it? Will this act contribute to the Kingdom?

• Satan will offer false representatives of the will of God, including astrologers, witches, mediums, false teachers, etc. We must scrupulously avoid these alternatives and "hold fast to that which is good."

• There will be times when the will of God will not be

abundantly clear to us. During those occasions we are expected to retain our faith and "wait on the Lord."

Ultimately, the comprehension of God's will requires a careful balance between rational deliberation on one hand, and emotional responses on the other. Each Christian must find that balance in his own relationship with God, yielding to the teachings of the Holy Spirit. One man's search for this understanding was expressed beautifully by the Reverend Everett Howard, a veteran missionary to the Cape Verde Islands. Here is his personal account of how he learned to put himself completely in the hands of God:

> I've spent thirty-six years in missionary service—a lifetime that has passed so quickly. About fifty years ago when I was just a young boy I knew that God was calling me, but I was confused. I didn't know just where or when or what He wanted me to do. Years passed and I went on through school and college and into Lincoln and Lee Dental University in Kansas City, Missouri. I was still fighting and battling away, unsure of God's direction for my life.
>
> One day I came to the point of a definite decision. My dad was a Christian and his prayers were inspirational. But that was secondhand, and I wanted something that could be mine—something I could take through life with me. So I went into the little church where my dad was pastoring and locked the doors so I could be alone. I guess I was ashamed for anyone to hear me pray, but that's the way it was. I knelt down at the little altar and took a piece of paper and a pencil and said, "Now this is going to be for life!"

I listed everything on that page. I filled it with promises of what I would do for God, including my willingness to be a missionary, and every possible alternative I could think of. I promised to sing in the choir and give my tithes and read the Bible and do all the things I thought God might want of me. I had a long list of promises and I really meant them.

Then when I had finished that well-written page, I signed my name at the bottom and laid it on the altar. There alone in the church I looked up and waited for "thunder and lightning" or some act of approval from the Lord. I thought I might experience what Saint Paul did on the road to Damascus, or something equally dramatic. I knew that God must be terribly proud of me—a young fellow who would make a consecration like that. But nothing happened. It was quiet, still and I was so disappointed.

I couldn't understand it, so I thought I must have forgotten something. I took out my pencil again and tried to think about what I'd left out. But I couldn't remember anything else. I prayed again and told the Lord that I had put everything possible on that paper. Still nothing happened, though I waited and waited.

Then it came. I felt the voice of God speaking in my heart. He didn't shout or hit me over the head. I just felt in my own soul a voice speak so clearly. It said, "Son, you're going about it wrong. I don't want a consecration like this. Just tear up the paper you've written."

I said, "All right, Lord." And I took the paper I had

written so carefully and wadded it up.

Then the voice of God seemed to whisper again, "Son, I want you to take a blank piece of paper and sign your name on the bottom of it, and let Me fill it in."

"Oh! oh! that's different, Lord," I cried. But I did what He said there at the altar in the little church.

It was just a secret between God and me, as I signed the paper. And God has been filling it in for the past thirty-six years.

Maybe I'm glad that I didn't know what was going to be written on the page. Things like . . . lying sick in the lonely mountains of the Cape Verde Islands, burning up with fever, with no medicine and no doctor, and the closest hospital more than 3,000 miles away. And the famine, when almost a third of the population in our part of the country had starved to death . . . money wasn't coming through . . . nine months without one single check or a penny . . . everything we owned had to be sold in order to live . . . that wasn't written on the page until the time came. But, you know, there was no depression. Those were the most blessed days, because God was there! And if I could turn around and do it again, I'd go every step of the way that we've traveled for the last thirty-six years.

To those who are listening to me tonight, I hope you will also put your name at the bottom of a blank sheet of paper and let God fill it in. Especially if you're worried about who you should marry or where to go to school or what training you should get, and all those questions which cause young people to struggle. You don't know the answers to such questions and neither do I. If I tried to tell you what to do it would probably be wrong. But God knows. Let Him fill in the page, regardless of where He leads or the difficulties you will experience. And of this I am absolutely confident: the Lord will make His purposes and plans known in plenty of time for you to heed them.

Reverend Howard retired after 36 years in the service of his Master. He affirmed that God was still writing on the page which he signed as a youth. For me, volumes of theological analysis cannot equal the wisdom in his words. I hope his story encourages you (as it has me) to sign a blank page and let God determine the direction your life will take.

LEARNING-DISCUSSION IDEAS

Why You Can't Trust Inner Feelings and Impressions

1. Reread the section "Can You Know God's Will?" Do you agree or disagree that Christians often attempt to determine God's will by their inner feelings and impressions? With a partner, discuss, Are feelings and impressions reliable? Look to personal experiences for evidence pro and con.

2. Identify areas of your life that are difficult for you when it comes to determining God's will. What encouragement do you find in Isaiah 41:10; 42:16; James 1:5; John 16:13?

3. What ideas for discerning between a false notion and a true leading from God do you find in the following Scriptures? Psalm 32:8-11; Proverbs 3:5-7; Jeremiah 33:3. From ideas in these Scripture references write three brief guidelines you should follow in seeking God's will.

4. Dr. Dobson states that impressions are often influenced by state of health, fatigue and overall feelings of self-worth (or lack of it). What does this say to you regarding when to make important decisions?

5. The following Scripture references help the Christian tell the difference between the leading of the Holy Spirit and the influences of Satan: Hebrews 2:18; Ephesians 1:16-19; 1 John 4:4; and Psalm 32:8. List promises and reassuring statements you find in these verses.

6. What is your response to the following true life situation? Jack was just completing a four-year tour of duty in the Navy as a reactor technician on a nuclear submarine. Back at base after completing his last three-month stint at sea, he received an offer of a generous bonus and further education if he signed up for an additional two years in the Navy.

Puzzled as to what to do, he and his wife talked and prayed. A few nights later he dreamed that he accepted the offer, was sent to San Diego to school and that both he and his wife were very unhappy.

"I guess it isn't God's will for us to go to San Diego," says Jack. What would you say to Jack. After you have finished working through all of the ideas in this learning-discussion guide think through Jack's situation again.

7. The psalmist prayed: "Teach me to do your will, for you are my God; may your good Spirit lead me on level

ground" (Ps. 143:10). Write your own prayer asking God about His will for specific areas and situations in your own life.

How to Test Inner Feelings and Impressions

1. Dr. Dobson calls attention to writings of Martin Wells Knapp who, in his book *Impressions,* says that one of Satan's traps is to get the Christian to accept his own feelings and impressions as the voice of God without any questions asked. Knapp says when this occurs "the devil has all he wants." Do you agree? Why? What goals does Satan have? (For ideas see 1 Pet. 5:8; Eph. 6:12; John 8:44.)

2. List the four steps Knapp gives for testing your impressions and feelings to determine if they are truly God's leading.

3. Do you agree or disagree with the statement: Guidance from the Lord is *always* in accordance with the Holy Scripture? Why? Do you feel the following Bible passages support this principle? How? With a partner or study group, discuss Romans 15:4; 1 Corinthians 10:11; Deuteronomy 12:32; 1 Peter 1:25; 2 Timothy 3:16; Psalm 119:105,130.

4. What do you discover as God's will for your life in the following Scriptures? First read Romans 12 and underline or list specifics that are God's will for your everyday life. Also, read 1 Thessalonians 5:11-22 for additional guidance concerning God's will.

5. According to author Knapp, a second important test for God's will is the matter of *rightness.* Can you identify one very strong personal desire you have at the present time? Have you attempted to think about it in

terms of God's will for you? First, how does your desire measure up to God's standards for you as revealed in Scripture? Second, how does your desire hold up when you confront it with the question, "Is this right?" What do you find in John 16:7-14 to help you discern right from wrong? Do you rely on the Holy Spirit for guidance? How? When? Can you remember a specific situation?

6. Step three in Knapp's testing of impressions and feelings is *providence*. The dictionary defines providence as: "divine guidance"; and the word providential as: "*occurring as if by an intervention of divine power.*" Have you personally experienced what you feel to be "providential circumstances"? With a partner, evaluate and discuss the importance of circumstances when it comes to determining God's will. Discuss together the following situation:

Sam wants to relocate in a different kind of job. He sees no scriptural reason why it would not be God's will. He has been watching the classified ads for weeks and even went to an employment agency, but no job of the kind he wants has turned up. If you were Sam would you feel changing jobs at this time was not God's will? How can Sam feel reassured that God does care about this situation? How does Joshua 1:9 apply? Also read Isaiah 43:2 and Matthew 28:20.

7. The last step in Knapp's exercise in determining God's will is asking yourself the question: Is it reasonable? Dr. Dobson says: "The apostle Paul referred to the Christian life as a 'reasonable service.' Accordingly, the will of God can be expected to be in harmony with *spiritually enlightened judgment.*"

With a partner or in a small group check through the

following list and choose words that have special meaning when it comes to deciding whether or not a course of action is reasonable. Can you add to this list?

abilities	*appropriate*
responsibilities	*God's standards*
interests	*intent*
educational background	*selfish or unselfish*
physical condition	*effect on family*
purpose	*now or later*

8. Dr. Dobson says: "I believe there are times in the lives of most believers when confusion and perplexity are rampant." He cites examples in the lives of Job (Job 23:3,8,9) and Abraham (Gen. 22). Can you think of situations in your own life when God's will seemed obscure and circumstances hard to understand?

9. Dr. Dobson deplores the shallow teaching that denies there are times in a Christian's life when God's will and plan of action are not clear. In fact, God's will does not always make sense to the Christian. What is your reaction to this? Do you agree or disagree that there are times when God's will, and the circumstances we find ourselves in, will be incomprehensible and confusing? What can we do? Do passages like Isaiah 55:8; James 1:2; Romans 8:28,35-39 give you any help? Why?

10. When do people most frequently seek the will of God? (a) When they want help in answering troublesome questions? (b) When they are faced with difficult choices such as where to live, which job to take, what school to choose, etc.? (c) When they want to harness God's power

for more successful living? (d) When they are seeking to understand if their personal plans and desires harmonize with God's purpose and plan? Of the four reasons, which is the most valid for trying to determine God's will? (See Rom. 12; Eph. 5:6-10,17.)

Notes

1. This and the following quotes are from Martin Wells Knapp, *Impressions* (Revivalist Publishing, 1892).

For Further Reading

Briscoe, D. Stuart. *Patterns for Power.* Ventura, CA: Regal Books, 1979. Guidance for examining your relationship with God and encouragement for living out what you are learning. From the parables of Luke.

Little, Paul. *Affirming the Will of God.* Downers Grove, IL: Inter-Varsity Press. n.d. Encouragement that the Christian can know God's will and purpose.

Myra, Harold. *The New You.* Grand Rapids: Zondervan Publishing House, 1973. What is God's will for the new Christian? Here are answers to some questions often asked about the "new life."

Ridenour, Fritz. *Lord, What's Really Important?* Ventura, CA: Regal Books, 1979. A solid biblical introduction to values. How do your values compare with the teachings of Christ and other parts of Scripture? What can you do to change or strengthen the values you already have?

Shoemaker, Sam. *Extraordinary Living for Ordinary Men.* Grand Rapids: Zondervan Publishing House, n.d. Inspiring examples of Shoemaker applying gospel truth to the practical business of daily living.

Wagner, C. Peter. *Your Spiritual Gifts Can Help Your Church Grow.* Ventura, CA: Regal Books, 1979. A thorough, practical look at spiritual gifts and how to find yours.